T0167762

DISCOVER

THE HIDDEN

LISTENER

A Project of the

ANNENBERG FOUNDATION TRUST
AT SUNNYLANDS

in Partnership with the

HOOVER INSTITUTION

DISCOVERING
THE HIDDEN

AN ASSESSMENT OF RADIO LIBERTY AND WESTERN BROADCASTING TO THE USSR DURING THE COLD WAR

A Study Based on Audience Research Findings, 1970–1991

R. Eugene Parta

Former Director of Audience Research and Program Evaluation
Radio Free Europe/Radio Liberty, Inc.

HOOVER INSTITUTION PRESS
Stanford University
Stanford, California

Hoover Institution Press Publication No. 546

First printing, 2007
13   13   12   11   10   09   08   07   9   8   7   6   5   4   3   2   1

Manufactured in the United States of America

The paper used in this publication meets the minimum requirements of the American National Standard for Information Sciences—Permanence of Paper for Printed Library Materials, ANSI Z39.48–1992.

Library of Congress Cataloging-in-Publication Data
Parta, R. Eugene, 1940–
Discovering the hidden listener : An assessment of Radio Liberty and western broadcasting to the USSR during the Cold War ; A study based on research findings, 1970–1991 / by R. Eugene Parta.
    p. cm.—(Hoover Institution Press publication ; no. 546)
Includes bibliographical references and index.
ISBN-10: 0-8179-4732-9
ISBN-13: 978-0-8179-4732-3
1. International broadcasting—Soviet Union. 2. Radio broadcasting—Soviet Union. 3. Radio audiences—Soviet Union. 4. Radio Liberty.
5. Voice of America (Organization) I. Title. II. Series.
HE8697.45.S65P37 2007
384.54′4—dc22   2006006444

CONTENTS

LIST OF FIGURES

ACKNOWLEDGMENTS

A special thanks is due the Bernard M. Osher Foundation of San Francisco for supporting a fellowship that funded my research in the archives at the Hoover Institution and Stanford University at various points in 2004–2005. I would also like to thank Elena Danielson and Amy Desai of the Hoover Institution for their support during my time there.

Thank you as well to A. Ross Johnson of the Hoover Institution and Radio Free Europe/Radio Liberty (RFE/RL), Mark Rhodes, Charlie Allen and James Critchlow, all of whom read and commented on a draft at various points in its gestation. Patricia LeRoy's editing was as deft as always. Needless to say, any remaining errors are my sole responsibility.

I owe a lasting debt to the patient mentoring I received from my predecessor, the late Dr. Max Ralis and to the late Professor Ithiel de Sola Pool of MIT who took me under his wing and introduced me to the mysteries of the world of computer simulation.

My wife, Lynne, and sons, Rolf and Max, put up with my many absences during the period covered by this analysis and have, over the years, shown amazing patience, acceptance and love. For that my heartfelt thanks.

PREFACE
August 1991:
The Coup, the White House and
Radio Liberty

". . . And during the 3–4 days of this coup, Radio Liberty was one of the very few channels through which it was possible to send information to the whole world and, most important, to the whole of Russia, because now almost every family in Russia listens to Radio Liberty . . ."

Russian President Boris Yeltsin speaking in a
special edition of Radio Liberty's
"In the Country and the World" program of
August 24, 1991

Perhaps Boris Yeltsin exaggerated when he said that every family in Russia listened to Radio Liberty during the August 1991 coup attempt, but he didn't overstate its significance. A survey carried out a few weeks after the coup by *Vox Populi,* a leading Moscow research institute, showed that 30% of Muscovites heard Radio Liberty during the crisis days of August, 19–21 most listening constantly or several times a day.[1] The figures were even higher among Moscow elites. Among the elite groups surveyed, an average of 43% turned to Radio Liberty for information on the crisis (40% of the People's Deputies, 28% of high government officials, 55% of political activists and an overwhelming 70% of media and cultural professionals).[2]

During the three crisis days Radio Liberty had provided unique coverage of events through two of its reporters holed up on the 11th floor of the White House, the Russian Parliament building which was under siege. They telephoned a steady stream of reports to Munich from where they were broadcast back to the Soviet Union on powerful un-jammed shortwave signals, providing detailed accounts from inside the coup's seat of resistance. Yeltsin's call for a general strike against the coup leaders was broadcast by Radio Liberty within minutes to all corners of the country. The extensive, newly-formed network of Radio Liberty stringers in Moscow and throughout Russia were on the job feeding information to broadcast headquarters in Munich, covering the entire political spectrum from coup opponents on the barricades to hard-line backers of the coup.[3]

Typewritten news bulletins entitled "Radio Liberty Informs . . ." were posted on walls around the barricades.[4] According to People's Deputy Oleg Adamovich, "In these days Radio Liberty was the most important source of information for the Soviet people."[5] USSR President Gorbachev said he relied on the broadcasts of Radio Liberty, the BBC and Voice of America for information on events in Moscow and reactions around the world during his three days of imprisonment at his Crimean dacha.[6]

For its role in informing the Soviet peoples during the coup, Russian President Yeltsin issued a decree on August 27, 1991, directing the authorities to permit Radio Liberty to open a permanent bureau and assign it office space in Moscow, accredit it throughout the Russian Republic and provide it with the necessary channels of communication.[7] The preamble states:

> "In connection with a request by the administration of Radio Free Europe/Radio Liberty, which is financed by the Congress of the United States of America, and taking into account its role in objectively informing the citizens of the RSFSR and the world at large about the course of the democratic processes in Russia, the events in the country and the world, the activities of the legal leadership of the RSFSR during the coup d'etat in the USSR, I decree:"

How did it happen that Radio Liberty—most vilified of Western broadcasters in the official Soviet press, target of relentless jamming during most of its existence—had amassed such a vast audience, who so trusted its broadcasts, that it was able to experience its finest hour defending the same democratic forces that it had nurtured over almost four decades of broadcasting? Once the pariah among Western broadcasters during the Cold War, Radio Liberty was now accepted as a legitimate participant on the Russian media scene by the authorities themselves.

That question has yet to be answered in all its complexity, although many books and articles have looked at the fascinating story of Radio Liberty, its early years and political history, its many colorful and exceptional personalities, and its multi-faceted, and in many ways unique, programming. This short study has a different perspective. It focuses on the listeners to Western radio and to Radio Liberty. How many of them were there? Who were they? Why did they listen? How did they listen? What did Western radio and Radio Liberty mean to them? Did they make a difference?

What follows here should be understand only as a broad quantitative overview of the topic. A subsequent study will treat the complex subject in significantly greater detail. Missing here is any real mention of the eloquent testimonials listeners gave in the interviews (and their many letters) on what the radios meant to them. That too must wait.

EXECUTIVE SUMMARY

1. The following study is based on more than 50,000 inter-
    views conducted with Soviet citizens traveling outside the
    USSR during the period 1972–1990, under the auspices
    of the Soviet Area Audience and Opinion Research Unit
    (SAAOR) of RFE/RL. Projections of Western radio audi-
    ence estimates on to the population of the USSR were
    done through the mass media computer simulation
    methodology developed at the Massachusetts Institute of
    Technology (MIT) and adapted to the requirements of
    RFE/RL.
2. The data show that audiences to Western radio in the
    USSR were large. In the period 1978–1990, the weekly
    reach of Western radio was in the range of 25% of the
    adult population. In 1989, Western radio was reaching ca.
    25 million people on an average day and over 50 million
    in the course of an average week.
3. From 1972 to 1988, Voice of America (VOA) had the
    largest audiences (with a weekly reach of around 15%
    of the adult population). Weekly audiences to BBC and
    Radio Liberty fluctuated between 5 and 10% of the adult
    population. Deutsche Welle audiences were in the 2–5%
    range.
4. When jamming ended on Radio Liberty in November
    1988, its audience immediately spiked, and in 1989–1990
    its weekly reach—at ca. 15–16%—was the highest of all

Western broadcasters to the USSR. It was reaching about 35 million people a week at this point.

5. Jamming had significant impact on the ability of Soviet citizens to listen to Western broadcasts. Intensification or cessation of jamming of Western radios was a barometer of East-West relations. Nonetheless, both broadcasters and listeners found ingenious ways to circumvent the jamming.

6. When surveys on Western radio listening were first able to be conducted within the USSR by Western clients, the results confirmed large audiences during the Cold War period and were largely consistent with SAAOR estimates. Internal surveys estimated that during the Cold War ca. 30–40% of the adult population had heard Western radio broadcasts.

7. Audiences to Western stations were dominated by urban males in the 30–50 years age range with at least secondary education. Listening rates were highest in Moscow, Leningrad, the Baltic States and the Trans-Caucasus. They were lowest in Central Asia, Moldavia and the provincial RSFSR. Interestingly, Communist Party membership, *per se,* was not a predictor of listening to Western radios. Party members and non-members listened at similar rates.

8. Personal political orientation, however, was a strong determinant of Western radio listening. Those who could be considered "Liberals" in the Soviet context listened most to Western radio and made up a majority of the audience to Radio Liberty, which was viewed as the most politically engaged station, given its focus on internal Soviet developments. "Moderates" also listened to Western radio at high rates, dominating the audiences to the other Western stations. "Conservatives" and "Hardliners" listened considerably less.

9. Western stations found a definite niche in the Soviet media environment during the Cold War. They were heard primarily for information, with entertainment playing a secondary motivational role according to SAAOR data (this might be a result of the methodology employed and differs somewhat from Soviet internal findings). They were sought out especially for information not available from the official media, and also as a check on that media,

to verify or refute information found there. Western radio listening had a high correlation with "word-of-mouth" communication, which meant that Western information was "amplified" to a far larger part of Soviet society than just the listening audience.

10. A number of case studies are examined in this paper to shed light on the role played by Western radio as an information source, and to determine what impact it might have had on attitude and opinion formation. Case studies on the war in Afghanistan (1979–1989), the *samizdat* phenomenon (1970s), the Korean Airliner incident (1983), the Chernobyl disaster (1986), *glasnost'* and *perestroika* (1985–1989) all demonstrate the importance of Western broadcasts in providing an alternative version of events and thereby contributing to attitudes that were at variance with those expressed by official Soviet media. The case study of attitudes to Solidarity in Poland (1990–1991), however, demonstrates the difficulty faced by Western radio when the Soviet population perceived itself to be under direct threat, and Soviet media played on their fears.

11. The question of validating the unorthodox methodology employed by SAAOR to study media and attitudinal patterns in the USSR is approached in several ways, primarily through comparisons with studies that were carried out either officially or unofficially in the USSR. This paper examines correlations between SAAOR studies on media use and internal Soviet studies on the topic and finds a strong congruence. It presents results of SAAOR survey data alongside those of unofficial polls carried out in the USSR on attitudes to Andrei Sakharov and to the Solidarity movement in Poland, and finds a striking similarity. Western media organizations were able to commission a few polls in the late *perestroika* period (1988–1989): these are compared with SAAOR findings, and again show essentially the same results. Estimates of listening to Western radio in SAAOR polls and in internal studies in 1990 also show a high degree of consistency. Findings from the traveler database of ca. 50,000 respondents are internally consistent with interviews conducted among ca. 25,000 Jewish emigrants from the USSR. While none of

these comparisons provide formal statistical proof of the validity of SAAOR data, they strongly reinforce the credibility and feasibility of SAAOR findings.

12. Analysis based on information from Soviet archives was presented for the first time at the Hoover–Wilson Center Conference in October 2004. The findings largely confirm SAAOR data on large audiences to Western radio in the USSR in the late 1970s early 1980s. It is apparent from these two different data sources—East and West—that Western broadcasts played an important, and at times, critical role in the path of the Soviet Union toward a freer society.

DISCOVERING

THE HIDDEN

LISTENER

AN ASSESSMENT OF RADIO LIBERTY AND WESTERN BROADCASTING TO THE USSR DURING THE COLD WAR

A Study Based on Audience Research Findings, 1970–1991

SECTION

Measuring the Audience to Western Broadcasters in the USSR

Survey data on Radio Liberty's audience during the coup crisis in August 1991 was available within days of the event. It showed widespread listening to the station. This was not the case during most of the station's history, when the Soviet Union was off limits to Western survey researchers. Western radio broadcasting was considered "ideological diversion" and any attempt at researching the audience for the benefit of a Western broadcaster would have been considered little short of espionage, especially in the case of Radio Liberty.

Given that it was impossible to carry out classic audience research within the USSR itself, second-best methods had to be employed. The fallback was to interview systematically travelers from the Soviet Union who were temporarily outside their country.[1] Beginning in the early 1970s, emigrants from the USSR, primarily Jewish, but also some ethnic Germans, were also interviewed. These research efforts were directed by the Soviet Area Audience and Opinion Research (SAAOR) unit of RFE/RL, located in Paris.[2] The actual interviewing was carried out by

The original draft of this study was prepared for the Conference on Cold War Broadcasting Impact held October 13–15, 2004 at the Hoover Institution, Stanford University, Stanford, California. The conference was co-organized by the Cold War International History Project, Woodrow Wilson International Center for Scholars, Washington, DC, and the Hoover Institution of Stanford University, with support from the Center for East European and Eurasian Studies, Stanford University, and the Open Society Archives, Central European University, Budapest.

independent research institutes in a neutral manner that did not prejudice results in favor of a single broadcaster. The data were relied upon by all the major Western broadcasters to the USSR for their basic estimates of audience size and listening behavior.

During the 1950s and 1960s, interviewing travelers produced primarily *ad hoc* anecdotal evidence of listening, which provided useful insights but permitted few general inferences. By the early 1970s, data collection had been systematized to the point that preliminary generalized estimates could begin to be made about audience size and composition. During the period 1972–1990, over 50,000 interviews with Soviet travelers were conducted and analyzed using a sophisticated mass media communications computer simulation model developed at the Massachusetts Institute of Technology (MIT).[3] Since that part of the Soviet population which was allowed to travel to the West was demographically and ideologically skewed, highly robust methods were required to counteract those biases. Travelers tended to be more male, more urban, more educated, more middle-aged and more likely to be members of the communist party than the population at large. While the MIT simulation program could correct for the demographic skew, there was no real way to correct for the fact that travelers had been carefully screened for loyalty to the Soviet state. This might have had an impact on their willingness to admit to listening to certain Western radio stations (such as Radio Liberty) that were considered ideologically antagonistic. While the focus of this paper is not on methodology *per se,* the complicated methodological issues involved in surveying a non-representative traveling population are briefly discussed in Appendix A. The underlying principles of the MIT mass media simulation program are dealt with in Appendix B. Methodological issues will be examined in more depth in a subsequent publication.

Throughout this paper, for reasons of convenience, the term "sample" will be used to refer to the Soviet traveler data. This does not mean to imply that the sample of travelers is a random, scientific sample in the usual sense of the term. It should rather be taken to mean a survey group reconstructed by the MIT simulation program in such a way as to be representative of the adult population of the USSR.

In addition to the traveler survey, an entirely separate project, also managed by SAAOR, surveyed over 25,000 legal emigrants from the USSR on their media habits before emigration. This research could be conducted with the straightforward administration of a detailed questionnaire. Emigrant data were not used for estimating audience size in the Soviet Union, but provided much useful detailed information on listening behavior and permitted cross-checks to validate the internal consistency of the traveler data. Another source of useful information for the radios, although it couldn't be used to estimate audience size, was listener mail. Thousands of letters were received over the years, and their many first-hand accounts of listening behavior, along with their positive or critical comments, were of inestimable value to the broadcast services. However, listener mail is beyond the scope of this study and awaits a separate analysis.

No claim is made that the research approach used by SAAOR during the Cold War produced results that would have been as accurate as surveys freely conducted within the USSR using state-of-the-art methodology. *All research findings in this study have to be understood within the limits of that caveat.* There are always limits to accuracy and when direct impediments are placed in the way of the research process those limits can be severe. The data, however, do provide a rather remarkable body of internally consistent findings with high face validity, and we feel confident that they offer valuable insights into the role played by Western radio during the Cold War period. Along with the data on media use, a considerable amount of attitudinal data was gathered. As the size and quality of the database increased in the 1980s, and analytical methods became more refined, our understanding of the listeners gained in depth and richness. Through the careful analysis of this extensive database, it became possible to provide broadcast management with crucial information allowing them to adapt programming in order to better meet listeners' needs and desires.

When the Cold War ended and research could be conducted within the USSR, and later in the successor states to the Soviet Union, it became clear that our earlier measurements and understanding of audience behavior were firmly grounded and no major reassessments were required. Subsequent surveys conducted inside Russia after the fall of the USSR bore out the finding of widespread listening to foreign radio stations during the Cold War period and their importance to the Soviet peoples.

This paper is based on the extensive data gathered from SAAOR traveler surveys and addresses the important questions of audience size and listening trends over time, the position Western radio occupied in the Soviet media environment, listeners' demographic traits and attitudinal tendencies, the evolution of the image of different Western broadcasters, and listeners' programming preferences. The role of Western radio in various crisis situations will be examined through a number of case studies. An additional section examines issues of data validation, drawing on comparisons with internal Soviet studies, both official and unofficial. Finally, some tentative observations will be made on the important question of the impact of Western radio and Radio Liberty *from the listeners' perspective.* Impact can be an elusive issue to quantify and it is imprudent, if not impossible, to isolate a single factor in any causal process. These difficulties notwithstanding, it is important to attempt to better understand what Radio Liberty and Western radio actually meant to their listeners, and how their influence may have inspired or reinforced other tendencies at work in the USSR in its fitful movement toward a freer society.

SECTION

Trends in Listening to Western Broadcasters in the USSR: 1970–1991

2.1. Early Attempts to Quantify the Audience to Western Radio: The 1970s

As noted above, research on listening to Western radio in the USSR was essentially anecdotal or based on listener mail until 1970, when systematic surveying of Soviet travelers to the West began. These initial survey data, however, were too unrepresentative of the Soviet population to permit general inferences concerning the size of audiences to the different Western broadcasters. It wasn't until 1973 that the MIT computer simulation methodology was applied to the data, and an attempt was made to project the survey data onto the larger population of the USSR.[1]

These initial rough projections, based on some 2,000 respondent cases from 1970–1972, showed VOA with the largest audience of all the Western broadcasters—a position it was to hold until jamming was lifted on Radio Liberty in November 1988. This first application of the MIT simulation estimated that on a "typical" day VOA reached about 6% of the Soviet adult population, followed by Radio Liberty at 2.8% and BBC at 1.5%. All "other stations" combined were estimated to reach 7.2%. Cumulative weekly reach estimates were 23% for VOA, 11% for Radio Liberty, 5% for BBC and 26% for the "others."

An important finding of this first attempt to quantify audiences showed that there was very little overlap between the two

American stations, VOA and Radio Liberty. To a large degree, the audience to each station was different, both in demographic terms and in language of listening. The audience to VOA was relatively young, about three-quarters urban, and about evenly split between men and women. Radio Liberty, on the other hand, had a somewhat older audience, less urban, slightly better educated and strongly represented in the Union Republics.[2] This was consistent with the program offer of each station. Although both stations had strong news orientations, VOA carried considerably more entertainment and U.S.-oriented programming, while Radio Liberty, as a "surrogate" broadcaster, focused on political and cultural aspects of its broadcast area, the USSR, and was on the air in more regional languages.

Although these first general findings were encouraging, subsequent survey data throughout the 1970s showed audiences listening at somewhat lower rates. It is difficult to determine whether the later figures indicated real shifts in audience size, or if they reflected improved data collection techniques that produced a demographically more diverse sample. Figure 1 shows weekly reach rates for the four major broadcasters: VOA, Radio Liberty, BBC and Deutsche Welle through the remainder of the 1970s.[3]

In the 1973–74 data, a now un-jammed BBC moved ahead of Radio Liberty in terms of weekly reach and VOA's audience estimate declined from the 1970–72 data. (From 1973 to 1980, only Radio Liberty was subject to heavy jamming. Jamming was lifted on VOA, BBC and Deutsche Welle in 1973 in the climate of détente.)

Given the development of surveying techniques and analytical methodology during the early and mid 1970s, it seems likely that the earliest estimates from 1970–1972 should best be viewed as general approximations. It was not until the late

	1973-74 N=2,438	1975-76 N=2,804	1977-78 N=2,256	1979-80 N=2,431
VOA	19%	19%	15%	15%
BBC	11%	8%	7%	8%
Radio Liberty	9%	6%	4%	7%
Deutsche Welle	5%	6%	6%	5%

FIGURE 1. Estimated Weekly Reach Rates for Major Western Broadcasters to USSR: 1973–1980

1970s, after survey methods had been improved to procure a more diverse sample, and the MIT computer simulation methodology had been further refined, that annual audience estimates could be used to determine listener trends with a high degree of confidence.[4] These estimates will be examined in more detail below.

2.2. Weekly Reach of Western Broadcasters: 1980–1990

This section will focus on tracking audiences to Western radios during the 1980–1990 period when annual data bases were larger, data collection had become more routinely systematized, and the MIT computer simulation software was more specifically adapted to the needs of SAAOR. Consequently, we have more confidence in these estimates than in those for the 1970s shown in Figure 1.

The cumulative weekly reach of the major Western broadcasters to the USSR for this period is shown in Figure 2. (Cumulative weekly reach is the percentage of the population reached in the course of an average week. It will be referred to simply as "weekly reach" hereafter.) A reasonably consistent

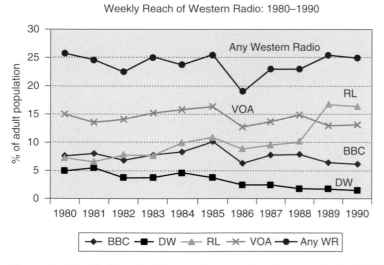

FIGURE 2. **Weekly Reach of Major Western Broadcasters in the USSR Among the Total Adult Population 16 Years and Older: 1980–1990**

pattern emerges throughout the period. The weekly reach of the combined Western broadcasters oscillated around 25%. VOA had the highest weekly reach, at around 15%, until it met direct competition from an un-jammed Radio Liberty in 1989. BBC was firmly anchored in the 5–10% range and Deutsche Welle hovered around 5% until 1986, when it began a slow but steady decline to around 2% in 1990.

The only station showing a major shift was Radio Liberty. The audience began a slow climb from ca. 7% in 1980 to ca. 10% in 1985, where it stayed until jamming ended in November 1988. At that point, its audience dramatically increased and, in terms of weekly reach, Radio Liberty became the leading Western broadcaster in terms of audience size in 1989 and 1990.

Of course neither the broadcasting nor the listening took place inside a vacuum. In order to better understand the dynamics of listening trends, it is important to view them against a double backdrop: on the one hand, Soviet jamming of the broadcasts, and on the other, events both inside and outside the USSR which might trigger increased interest in listening. Issues such as improvements in transmission capabilities or changes in programming emphasis are beyond the scope of this paper.

2.3. The Impact of Jamming

In the context of the Cold War, the USSR was disinclined to allow their citizens free access to what they called Western "voices." Jamming of VOA transmissions started on February 3, 1948 and BBC on April 13, 1948.[5] Jamming was to be a major weapon of the Soviet government against Western broadcasts throughout the Cold War period and its interruption or intensification served as a barometer of the East-West political climate. Jamming was lifted on VOA and BBC in June 1963, during the period of relaxation of tensions in the aftermath of the Cuban Missile Crisis and negotiations on the nuclear test ban treaty.[6] Jamming was resumed in August 1968 during the Warsaw Pact invasion of Czechoslovakia. It was halted again in 1973 during the period of détente, only to resume in 1981 at the time of declaration of martial law in Poland. Jamming was definitively ended on BBC transmissions in January 1987, and on VOA in

May 1987, during the period of *perestroika*. Selective jamming of Deutsche Welle started in August 1962 and continued until June 1963. It recommenced during the Czech crisis of August 1968, and the jamming pattern from that point on followed that of BBC and VOA. Radio Liberty was jammed without interruption from its first day on the air in March 1953 until November 22, 1988, and it was the number one target of the Soviet jamming network.[7]

Radio Sweden was subject to some early selective jamming which soon ended. A similar pattern was noted for Radio Canada International, which suffered only occasional selective jamming. Radio France International did not report jamming of its signals.

It is interesting to note the overall decline, as measured by SAAOR, in the weekly reach of all Western stations, from 25.6% in 1985 to 18.9% in 1986. If SAAOR's lower ratings for Western broadcasters were replicated by secret internal polls, the Soviet authorities may have felt that in the *perestroika/glasnost'* climate it was safe to end jamming on VOA, BBC and Deutsche Welle, since their audiences were already in decline. A jamming halt could be a major public relations benefit in the West, and signal a new climate of openness and confidence within the USSR. As noted, jamming

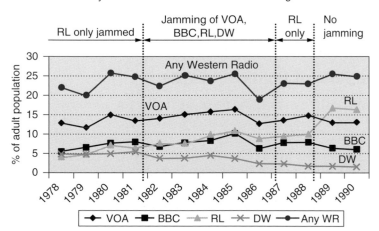

FIGURE 3. Weekly Reach of Western Broadcasters and Jamming: 1978–1990

ended on BBC in January 1987 and on VOA and Deutsche Welle in May 1987. Radio Liberty was apparently considered a more serious problem, for intense jamming was to continue another eighteen months.

When jamming ended on Radio Liberty in November 1988, its listening rates immediately shot upwards. By the second half of 1989, SAAOR's estimate of weekly reach was 16.8%, compared to 10% in 1988 under jamming (the latter being a relatively high figure in the circumstances).

While jamming certainly made listening to Western broadcasts in the USSR more difficult, it was not successful in preventing it altogether. Both broadcasters and listeners found ingenious ways of circumventing jamming,[8] and jamming may have had the unintended effect of increasing interest in the broadcasts in line with the maxim "forbidden fruit is often sweeter." At the height of the Cold War, the USSR had constructed such an extensive jamming transmitter network that it cost considerably more to jam Western broadcasts than to broadcast them.[9]

A study conducted by SAAOR in the early 1980s showed that respondents' listening habits were significantly affected by jamming.[10] About half the listeners in the sample (51%) reported that they tuned in Western stations less frequently than before August 1980, when all but Radio Liberty were un-jammed. They also stayed tuned for shorter periods of time. Even though the weekly reach levels of 1980 had been regained by 1984, listeners were tuning in less frequently in the course of a week and hearing fewer programs under difficult listening conditions.

2.4. The Role of Political Events

Political and other events were another factor influencing listening to Western broadcasts. Since surveying was carried out on a continual basis, not timed specifically to correspond to breaking events, it's not always possible to find a direct correlation between current events and increased or decreased listening, but some broad trends are apparent. Figure 4 shows weekly reach rates of Western radio in alignment with certain political events in the period 1978–1990.

Audiences began to build after the Soviet invasion of Afghanistan in 1979, and reached a peak in 1980 around the

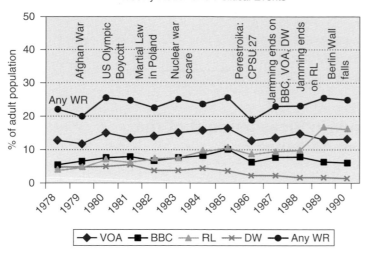

FIGURE 4. **Weekly Reach of Western Radio and Some Political Events**

time of the US Olympic boycott. They declined only slightly through the period of martial law in Poland, which was decreed in December 1981, and increased again in 1983 at the time when the US introduced Pershing missiles in Europe to counter the deployment of Soviet SS-20 missiles. A major media campaign attacking the US initiative was mounted in the Soviet press at this time, and it had the presumably unintended backlash effect of creating a war scare in the USSR.[11]

Overall listening rates remained fairly stable as Gorbachev ascended to the post of General Secretary of the CPSU in 1985. As noted above, they dropped considerably during the early *perestroika/glasnost'* period when Soviet media became livelier, and less fettered by official censorship. Listening rates to Radio Liberty dropped somewhat less than those of other stations at this time. Radio Liberty's focus on internal Soviet affairs may have made it increasingly relevant to its listeners as the political situation in the Soviet Union entered a period of growing ferment.

As jamming ended in 1987 (VOA, BBC, Deutsche Welle) and 1988 (Radio Liberty), weekly listening rates began to climb. The USSR was going through a period of lively internal debate, and Soviet citizens sought additional analysis and perspective from the Western "voices." If the Soviet leadership had gambled that lifting jamming on Western radios would have little impact on listening, they lost their bet in the short term, especially in the case of Radio Liberty. Overall audiences to Western radio returned close to 1980 and 1985 levels, and Radio Liberty overtook VOA as the leading Western broadcaster to the USSR. Audiences stayed high through the fall of the Berlin wall and through 1991, after which they began to recede.

2.5. Trends in Measurement of the "Core Audience"

Thus far we have been looking at the weekly reach of Western radios in terms of the total adult (16 years and older) population of the USSR. In 1986, SAAOR began to focus on listening within a subset of the total population where the sample data was strongest. This was in order to more accurately calibrate listening trends for internal reporting purposes.

Most listeners to Western radio belonged to that segment of the population which lived in urban areas and had at least a secondary education. For shorthand purposes, this has been designated the "core audience," which in many ways corresponded to the "target audience" for Western radio. Figure 5 shows listening trends among this "core audience" group (the referent population for the "core audience" in 1990 was 47.3 million people,

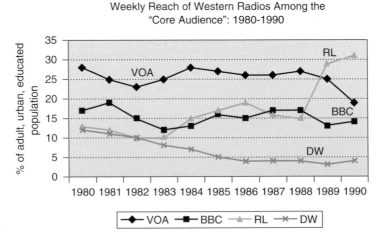

Weekly Reach of Western Radios Among the "Core Audience": 1980-1990

FIGURE 5. **Weekly Reach of Western Stations Among the "Core Audience" (Adult, Urban, Educated Population) in the USSR: 1978–1990**

compared to 209.8 million for the total adult population). Weekly listening rates are about double those shown in Figure 2 for the entire adult population.

The overall listening patterns noted for the "core audience" are essentially consistent with those noted for the total adult population earlier, although listening takes place at higher rates and shifts are more sharply delineated.

2.6. Listening to Western Broadcasts in the Last Years of the USSR: 1989–1991

As noted, after the final cessation of jamming of Radio Liberty in 1988, audiences to Radio Liberty rose sharply in 1989, even though overall listening to Western radio increased only slightly. Figure 6 shows clearly the changes that took place between 1988 and 1990, with a major increase in listening to Radio Liberty and minor decreases in listening to the other stations. Most of the new listeners to Radio Liberty came at the expense of other Western broadcasters, although some were genuinely new listeners to Western radio.

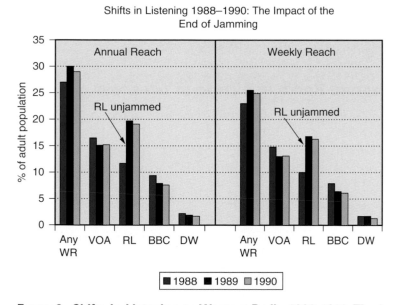

FIGURE 6. **Shifts in Listening to Western Radio 1988–1990. The Impact of the End of Jamming on Radio Liberty**

In 1989, completely new listeners to the station accounted for about 16% of Radio Liberty's audience.[12] A substantial majority of these new listeners heard Radio Liberty exclusively in Russian, the only language service to benefit from round-the-clock broadcasts. Although these new listeners resembled the station's long-term listeners in being urban and educated, there was evidence that there were more women among the new listeners and more younger people (under 30 years of age) than in the traditional audience which had built up under conditions of jamming.

Although newcomers to the Western radio audience in 1989 chose Radio Liberty in preference to other Western stations, it was clear that it would not be easy to gain their long-term loyalty. They tended to be more critical of the broadcasts than long-term listeners, and they tuned in for shorter time spans. Their main priority was to seek out information on the USSR, an area where Radio Liberty had an advantage over other Western broadcasters. There may also have been an urge to taste the "forbidden fruit" as well. However, as domestic media improved, many of these new listeners tended to gravitate back to indigenous media sources. But in the midst of the tumultuous events of 1989, Radio Liberty provided these newcomers with a context in which to make sense of conflicting information, as well as guidance in evaluating information from Soviet sources, and a fresh perspective on events.

2.7. Western Radio in a Time of *Glasnost'*

The policy of *glasnost'* in the media was one of the key elements of Gorbachev's *perestroika* and perhaps the one that was most visible to many Soviet citizens. *Glasnost'* presented both new challenges and new opportunities for Western broadcasters to the USSR.[13]

Soviet television during this time adopted a number of changes in programming and presentation intended to make TV broadcasts livelier and more interesting, and as a result they became more competitive with Western radio. At the same time they became an increasingly important source of information for Soviet citizens. This topic will be dealt with in more detail in the next section.

The central press was in the forefront of *glasnost,'* both in reporting on previously taboo subjects, and in serving as a forum for discussion of reform proposals. Under looser regime control than the electronic media, the Soviet press was no longer monolithic.

Although they were no longer the sole source of alternative viewpoints on Soviet issues, Western radios were now able to go beyond an observer's role and participate in the ongoing internal debate by providing critical but constructive analysis of Soviet affairs. Many topics remained outside the limits of *glasnost'* and Soviet citizens continued to turn to Western radio for information and analysis still unavailable from domestic media.

A study conducted somewhat earlier in 1987 showed that about one in five Western radio listeners said their listening behavior had changed because of *glasnost'*.[14] Of these, 65% were listening more frequently, 20% were listening with a more critical ear, and 15% were tuning in less frequently (see Figure 7).

Data from 1988 indicated that Western radio broadcasts continued to play an important role in informing Soviet citizens, despite growing confidence in domestic media.[15] Of the 5,032 respondents in the un-weighted sample, 55% used Western radio as an information source, and three-quarters of these listeners considered it an important source of information.

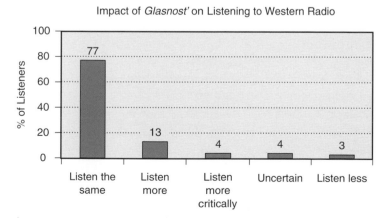

FIGURE 7. **Impact of *Glasnost'* on Listening to Western Radio**

2.8. Audience Cumulation Patterns: How Frequently Did Listeners Tune In?

Figure 8 shows audience cumulation patterns to Western radios in 1980, at a time when only Radio Liberty was subject to jamming. On a typical day, ca. 8% of the adult population was reached by a Western radio broadcast. This increased to about a quarter of the adult population reached in the course of an average week, and just over 30% in an average month. The annual reach of Western radio was only slightly higher than the monthly reach, at about a third of the adult population. Most listeners to Western radio were reached during the course of a month with relatively little increment after that point. This suggests that most listeners were serious and tuned in fairly frequently, rather than just dial-twiddlers who might come across a station by chance from time to time. The weekly reach rate was approximately triple the daily reach rate, which indicates that the average listener tuned in Western stations about 2.2 times in an average week.

The pattern was somewhat different in 1989 when none of the radios was jammed (see Figure 9). Here the cumulation curve for "any Western radio" is flatter in its growth, going from ca. 12% on an average day to ca. 25% in an average week and ca. 27% in an average month.

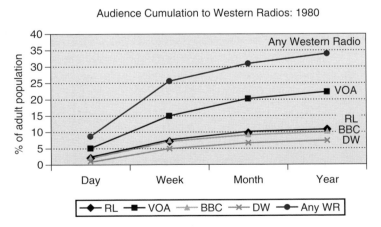

FIGURE 8. **Audience Cumulation Patterns in 1980 (Only Radio Liberty Jammed)**

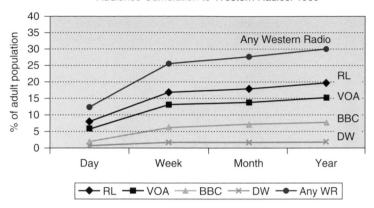

FIGURE 9. **Audience Cumulation Patterns in 1989 Post-Jamming**

In 1989, the average weekly reach was only about double the average daily reach. This indicates more frequent listening. In 1989, the average listener to any Western radio tuned in approximately 3.4 times a week, about half as much again as in 1980 under jamming. Most listeners did not tune in Western radio on a daily basis, but many of them listened very frequently indeed by 1989. Western radio reached most of its listeners in the course of an average week. The annual cumulation figure was only 5 percentage points higher, and was thus lower in 1989 than in 1980. To sum up, the audience to Western radio in an un-jammed, *glasnost'*-influenced environment in 1989 tuned in more frequently, even though its aggregate number was smaller.

2.9. Audience Duplication Patterns in the "Core Audience"

The first MIT simulation of the SAAOR data in the early 1970s showed that there was relatively little duplication on a daily basis in the audiences to VOA and Radio Liberty. In the course of a week, however, duplication rates rose as listeners found time to seek out other stations.

Under conditions of jamming, listeners would often have to settle for listening to whichever station had the most audible signal at a given moment. The cessation of all jamming in 1989

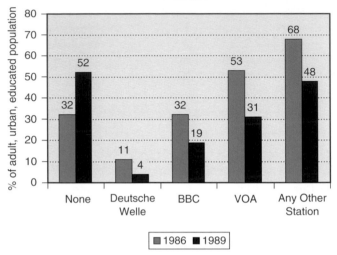

FIGURE 10. Duplication: Percentage of Radio Liberty's Weekly Audience Listening to Other Western Radios

brought a change in this pattern for Radio Liberty. Figure 10 shows the percentage of Radio Liberty's weekly audience which listened to other Western broadcasters during the same week among the "core audience," i.e. the adult, urban educated portion of the population.[16] In 1986 all stations were subject to jamming, and in 1989 none of them was any longer jammed.

In 1986, under jamming, two-thirds of Radio Liberty listeners heard another Western broadcaster in the course of the same week, most frequently VOA (about half), and BBC (about a third). About one-third of Radio Liberty's weekly audience listened solely to Radio Liberty and did not tune in other Western radios.

The end of jamming in 1989 brought about a significant change in this pattern. In 1989, over half of Radio Liberty's audience in the "core population" restricted its Western radio listening to this one station. About three in ten Radio Liberty listeners also tuned in VOA and about two in ten heard BBC in the course of the same week. This would indicate a relatively high degree of loyalty to Radio Liberty among its listeners, over half of whom felt their informational needs were sufficiently met by this one station.

2.10. Listening in the Geographic Regions of the USSR: Overall Patterns in 1989

By 1988–1989, annual sample sizes had grown to a level (5,233 in 1988 and 4,593 in 1989) where it became possible to improve the methodology for deriving listening estimates for different regions of the USSR.[17] Although these estimates are less robust than the aggregate estimates for the entire USSR, they do provide insight on how listening was distributed across the country, and on the impact of broadcasting in the nationality languages. Figure 11 gives a regional breakdown of weekly listening to the

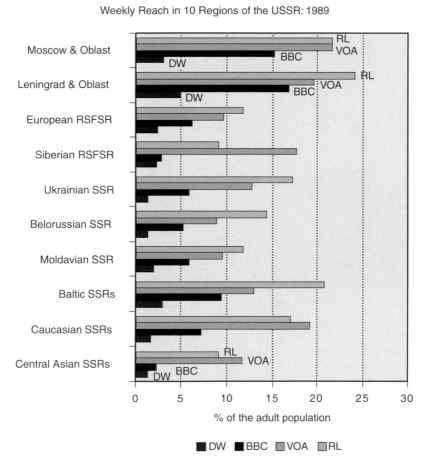

Weekly Reach in 10 Regions of the USSR: 1989

% of the adult population

■ DW ■ BBC ▨ VOA ▢ RL

FIGURE 11. Weekly Reach of Western Radio in Ten Regions of the USSR: 1989

major stations for 1988 and 1989. The increases shown in listening to Radio Liberty in 1989 are undoubtedly due to the cessation of jamming in November 1988, which will be examined in more detail in a subsequent chart.[18]

Figure 11 refers to listening in any language and does not distinguish between listening in Russian and in the nationality languages. While all four broadcasters were on the air in Russian, only Radio Liberty and VOA broadcast extensively in the nationality languages of the USSR (RFE/RL broadcasts in Estonian, Latvian and Lithuanian were under the RFE name. For the sake of convenience they will be included in the Radio Liberty figures in the following chart.)[19] Consequently, Radio Liberty and VOA had an advantage over BBC and Deutsche Welle in the non-Russian areas.

Radio Liberty drew its highest listening rates in the politically-charged centers of Moscow and Leningrad. It was conside rably less heard in the provincial European and Siberian parts of the RSFSR. In the non-Russian areas, its reach was highest in the Baltic States, where nationalist feeling ran high, Ukraine, the Trans-Caucasus and to a slightly lesser extent in Belorussia. Rates were lower in Moldavia and Central Asia.

VOA also showed a high rate of listening in Moscow and Leningrad. In the Siberian RSFSR, where the listening rate was also high, it may have benefited from a stronger short-wave signal than the other broadcasters. It led Radio Liberty by a short head in the Trans-Caucasus and Central Asia, but showed lower rates in the Baltic States, Ukraine and Belorussia (VOA did not broadcast in the Belorussian language).

BBC again had high rates in Moscow and Leningrad, but trailed significantly in other areas, with the exception of the Baltic States, where its Russian language broadcasts had a strong following. Deutsche Welle displayed a similar pattern but with lower overall rates.

2.11. Shifts in Listening to Radio Liberty After Cessation of Jamming

With the end of jamming in November 1988, the greatest upward shifts in listening to Radio Liberty took place in Moscow and Leningrad, where jamming had been heaviest

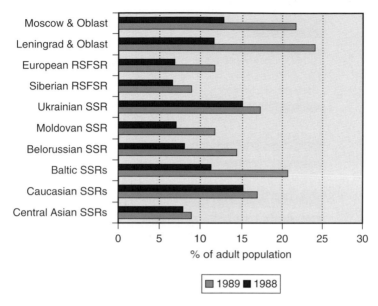

Shifts in Listening to RL in 10 Regions After the End of Jamming in Nov. 1988

FIGURE 12. Weekly Reach of Radio Liberty in Ten Regions of the USSR: 1988–1989. The Impact of Cessation of Jamming of RL

and most effective (see Figure 12). A large increase was also noted for the Baltic States, which were in an advanced state of nationalist effervescence. Listening increases were considerably less in Ukraine, the Trans-Caucasus and Central Asia.

2.12. Listening in Russian and Nationality Languages: RL and VOA

During the Cold War, Radio Liberty's Russian service played the role of an all-Union service with round-the-clock broadcasting. The smaller nationality language services had far fewer broadcast hours. Anecdotal evidence suggested that they complained of weaker short-wave signals as well, though this latter point was difficult to monitor and verify. This situation put the nationality language services at a certain disadvantage with regard to the Russian service, even though they had the advantage of communicating in the local language and benefiting from nationalist

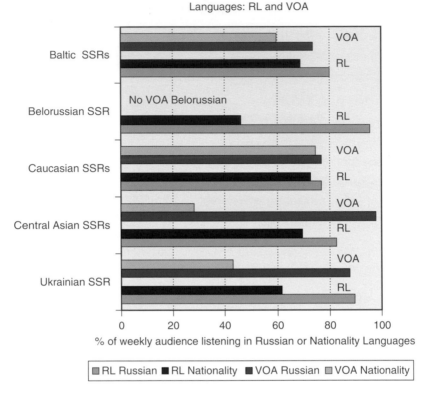

Listening in Russian and Nationality
Languages: RL and VOA

% of weekly audience listening in Russian or Nationality Languages

▣ RL Russian ■ RL Nationality ■ VOA Russian ▣ VOA Nationality

FIGURE 13. Listening in Russian and Nationality Languages: Radio Liberty and Voice of America 1989

sentiments. Figure 13 shows listening in Russian and nationality languages for Radio Liberty and VOA, the primary broadcasters in the nationality languages of the USSR.

In fact, it was commonplace for many of these respondents to listen in both Russian and a nationality language, as the combined totals above indicate. In all areas, however, audiences to the Russian language broadcasts were larger than in the nationality language.

For Radio Liberty, the highest rates of nationality language listening compared to Russian were found in the Trans-Caucasus, the Baltic States and Central Asia. They were somewhat lower in Ukraine, which has a large Russian-speaking population, and in Belorussia, where Russian is more widely spoken than Belorussian.

Voice of America showed a similar pattern, with the exception of Central Asia. In 1989 it broadcast only in Uzbek, while RL broadcast in five Central Asian languages. Most listening to VOA in Central Asia took place in the Russian language.

2.13. The Overall Annual Audience to Western Radio: 1980–1990

Regular listeners to Western radio were supplemented by those who tuned in only occasionally, often in response to specific events. Combining the weekly audience and the occasional audience gives the total annual reach of the broadcaster.

Figure 14 shows the total annual reach of each of the major Western broadcasters to the USSR. These figures indicate the potential for audience expansion during times of major crisis. The annual reach curves for individual stations follow a similar pattern to the weekly reach curves, but at higher rates.

As was noted earlier for weekly reach, the aggregate annual audience to Western radio broadcasts dropped sharply from 1985 to 1986 and then increased in 1987 and 1988 when jamming was removed in two stages. However, the higher annual reach rates noted in 1980 and 1985 were never regained. In 1990 SAAOR

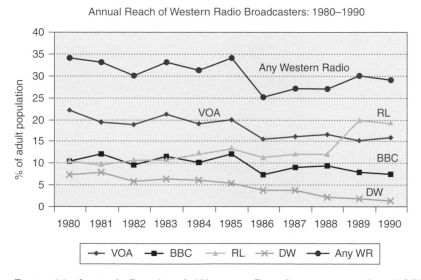

FIGURE 14. **Annual Reach of Western Broadcasters to the USSR: 1980–1990**

estimated that ca. 29% of the adult population of the USSR was being reached on at least an occasional basis by Western radio.

While these percentages were high, they did not do justice to the actual number of people being reached. In 1989–1990, Western radio was reaching ca. 25 million people on an average day and over 50 million in the course of a week. At this point, it does not seem unjustified to speak of a critical mass of the population of the USSR who were receiving information on the Soviet Union and on the world from Western radio.

2.14. Comparison with Internal Surveys to Confirm Audience Estimates

In 1991, it became possible to conduct surveys on Western radio listening inside the USSR, and later the Russian Federation, using local research institutes. The first surveys conducted bore out our earlier estimates of a large aggregate audience to Western broadcasts during the Cold War period.

Surveys conducted by Russian research institutes in the early 1990s suggested that up to half of the adult population had been reached at one time or another by Western broadcasters during the Cold War. This was an important confirmation of the findings of SAAOR research, and of the impact that the stations made during that period.

Figure 15 shows the percentage of people who said that they had "ever listened" to a given Western broadcaster. (Included here are VOA, BBC, Radio Liberty and Deutsche Welle.)[20] In 1992, in a survey conducted by the Institute of Sociology at the Russian Academy of Sciences (ISAN), those who said they had "ever listened" to a specific Western station ranged from ca. 30% to ca. 55% (these figures are not included in Figure 15). These rates were somewhat lower in a 1992 survey conducted by Vox Populi and in 1993–1994 surveys conducted by another leading Moscow institute, ROMIR.[21] Even if one were to hypothesize that the 1992 survey rates may have been on the high side (and possibly affected by exceptionally high listening during the August 1991 coup), the 1993 rates of "ever listened" to Western broadcasters, which fluctuated in more or less the same range through the end of 1999, would put the range of the Cold War audience between 30%–40% (or even higher, given that overlap in listening to stations is not total).

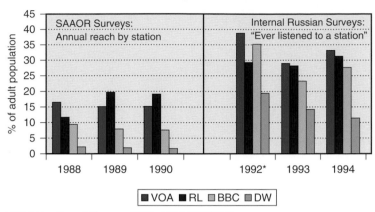

Comparison of SAAOR and Internal Russian
Surveys: 1988–1994

*1992 Vox Populi Survey, 1993–1994 ROMIR Surveys

FIGURE 15. Comparison of Findings from SAAOR Surveys 1988–1990 and Russian Surveys 1992–1994

Findings on annual reach for the major Western broadcasters in SAAOR traveler surveys in 1998–1990 all fit comfortably within the results from internal Russian surveys conducted in 1992, 1993 and 1994 on those who had "ever listened" to a given station. This increases our confidence that the earlier SAAOR estimates were credible and reasonable.

SECTION THREE

Who Were the Listeners and What Did They Hear?

3.1. Demographic Characteristics of Listeners to Radio Liberty

Both Western radio in general and Radio Liberty in particular showed their greatest relative appeal among males with a secondary or higher education living in urban areas.[1] It can be argued that this description also fits those most likely to be interested in politics, as well as those owning radio receivers capable of picking up a signal through jamming. This profile also corresponds to the type of programming carried by Western radio, which apart for some music programs targeted at youth was designed primarily for an urban intelligentsia.

The following charts (Figures 16–19) show weekly listening trends to Radio Liberty among different demographic groups from 1980 through 1989, the first year the station benefited from an un-jammed signal.

Men dominated Radio Liberty audiences throughout. It's noteworthy that the lifting of jamming at the end of 1988 led to a doubling of the listening rates of both the male and female audiences.

The relative appeal of Radio Liberty to different age groups shows an interesting shift throughout the 1980s (see Figure 17).

In 1980, at a time when increasing Soviet engagement in Afghanistan led to the US boycott of the Moscow Olympics, the highest weekly rate of listening to Radio Liberty was among

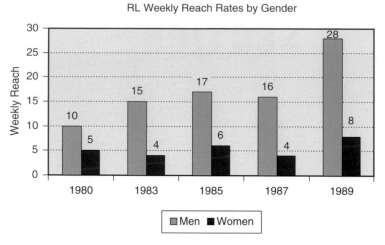

FIGURE 16. **Weekly Reach of Radio Liberty by Gender: 1980–1989**

those under 30 years of age. In 1983, the highest listening rate returned to the 30–49 year group, where Radio Liberty's appeal was always traditionally strongest, while the younger group dropped by more than half. In 1985, younger listeners came back, but the 30–49 year group remained dominant. In 1987, when jamming ended on VOA and BBC, the younger group again left Radio Liberty, presumably for the un-jammed stations. In 1989, with an un-jammed signal, listening rates among

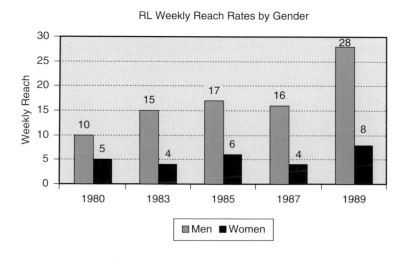

FIGURE 17. **Weekly Reach of Radio Liberty by Age: 1980–1989**

RL Weekly Reach Rates by Education

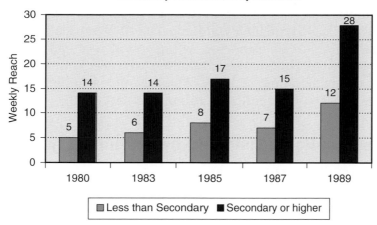

FIGURE 18. Weekly Reach of Radio Liberty by Education: 1980–1989

the young more than doubled, while listening rates among the 30–49 year group and the over-fifties increased, but not quite as dramatically.

Listening rates by education showed a consistent trend throughout the 1980s. People with secondary or higher education usually listened at rates about twice as high as those with lower educational levels (see Figure 18). The highest rates of all were found among those with higher education.

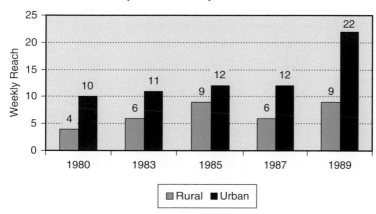

FIGURE 19. Weekly Reach of Radio Liberty by Rural or Urban Residence: 1980–1989

After cessation of jamming, weekly rates among the "educated" almost doubled from 15% in 1988 to 28% in 1989.

Despite the fact that audibility of Radio Liberty was usually better in rural than in urban areas, the station appealed essentially to an urban audience. For one thing, educational levels were higher in urban areas, for another, Radio Liberty's programming was essentially targeted at an educated urban audience.

3.2. Western Radio Listening by Attitudinal Type

It is hardly surprising that personal political orientation was a major determinant of Western radio listening. Not only was this an important predictive indicator of listening to Western radio, it also correlated in different ways with specific international broadcasters.

In 1984, SAAOR published an attitudinal typology of urban Soviet citizens based on over 3,000 interviews with Soviet travelers to the West in the late 1970s and early 1980s.[2] Five questions, determined on the basis of a factor analysis, provided a scale that broadly segmented the population on a spectrum from "hardline" to "liberal" according to their attitudes toward civil liberties in the USSR. Figure 20 gives the breakdown of the urban population of the USSR in terms of these five attitudinal types.

"Liberals" and "hardliners" were at roughly equal strength in the urban population, with one in eight subscribing to one or

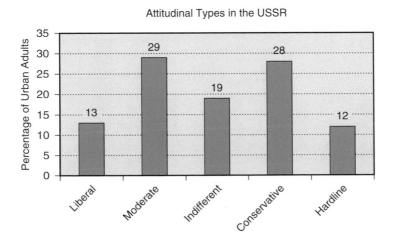

FIGURE 20. Attitudinal Types in the USSR (Urban Population)

the other position. "Moderates" and "Conservatives" mirrored each other as well, with approximately three in ten in each camp. About one in five urban Soviet citizens could be classified as "indifferent" or neutral, holding down the center of the scale.

In terms of media use, the "liberals" were significantly more likely to be listeners to Western radio than any of the other types. Almost 80% of the group said that they listened to the broadcasts (see Figure 21).

"Liberals" used word-of-mouth as an information source at higher rates than any other group, suggesting that information gathered from Western radio sources received an amplifier effect by being passed on through word-of-mouth communication. "Moderates" also used word-of-mouth communications at relatively higher rates than their more conservative counterparts, again giving a booster effect to the messages conveyed by Western broadcasters. "Hardliners" tended to rely on domestic TV as their main information source and made little use of Western radio broadcasts.

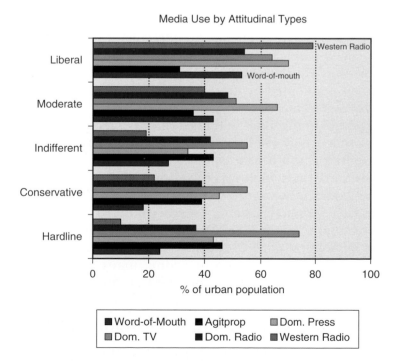

FIGURE 21. Media Use by Attitudinal Types in the USSR

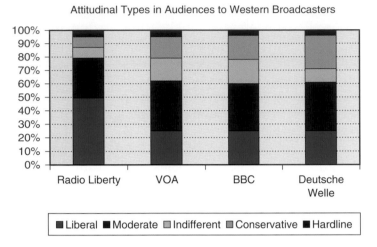

FIGURE 22. **Audiences to Western Broadcasters by Attitudinal Type**

The individual Western stations attracted different types of listeners in terms of political orientation. Figure 22 shows that half of Radio Liberty's audience was composed of "liberals," and that another 30% were "moderates," giving it a sharper ideological profile than the other major broadcasters. In light of the more hard-edged political broadcast style of Radio Liberty this is not surprising. The audiences to VOA, BBC and Deutsche Welle were all dominated by "moderates," who outnumbered the "liberals" two to one in the urban population.

These findings imply that if Radio Liberty had wanted to increase its audience in 1984, an apparent strategy might have been to re-position the broadcasts to increase their appeal to "moderates." Since the station was the prime target of the Soviet jamming network, however, this seems problematic, given that only the most committed listeners were willing to make the extra effort to tune in through constant intense jamming. A blunting of its political edge could have cost Radio Liberty listeners among the "liberals" without adding many among the "moderates," who listened to the other western broadcasters.

3.3. Motivations for Listening to Western Radio

As their primary motivation for tuning in Western radio broadcasts, Soviet respondents to the SAAOR traveler surveys cited the desire to hear uncensored news, followed by the need to

Motivations for Listening to Western Radio: 1985

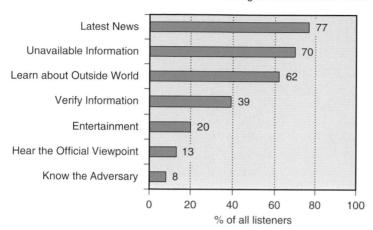

% of all listeners

FIGURE 23. **Motivations of Soviet Citizens for Listening to Western Radio Broadcasts: 1985**

obtain information not available from sources within the USSR (see Figure 23).[3] A third reason was to learn first-hand about the outside world from non-Soviet sources. Another important motive was to verify or disprove information already received from the Soviet media. Seeking entertainment was also a motivation for listening but, at 20%, it ranked relatively low in the SAAOR traveler surveys. This may underestimate the real interest of Soviet audiences in the music and entertainment programs of Western radios. Listener mail to these programs was considerable, and there is a great deal of anecdotal evidence attesting to their popularity. The relatively low rating for entertainment in the traveler surveys may be an artifact of the methodology. Travelers as a group were likely to be much more interested in politics than the average Soviet citizen, while younger people who listened heavily to music programs were less likely to be able to travel outside the USSR.

Hearing the "official viewpoint," a category usually reserved for government-sponsored stations such as VOA, BBC and Deutsche Welle, was important to about one in seven listeners. A few claimed that they listened to Western broadcasts in order to better understand their Western "adversaries." Whether this was a genuine motivation, or merely a disingenuous response, is difficult to gauge, but it was a reason occasionally cited, notably by Communist Party members.

As categories are not always comparable, specific motivations for listening from previous surveys are not given here, but they follow the same basic pattern. Information always scored much higher than entertainment as a primary motivation for listening. Survey data from 1987 showed that 91% of respondents said they listened to get information of various kinds, while only 13% noted entertainment as a primary motive.[4] It's noteworthy that in the *perestroika* year of 1987 13% claimed "moral support" as a motivation for listening to Western broadcasts.

Motivations for listening to specific stations generally followed this basic pattern, with a few important nuances. Radio Liberty was singled out for its coverage of the USSR and its nationality programming, and was also used as a way to verify domestic Soviet information, or to get otherwise unavailable information. VOA was often cited for its coverage of the West and generally high quality programming, including entertainment shows, while BBC was noted for its "objectivity."

3.4. Choice of Programming from Radio Liberty

In terms of the type of programming they preferred to hear on Radio Liberty, listeners invariably selected the latest news, and information focused on the USSR. However, in the decade spanning the period 1975 to 1986, from the time of the Brezhnev *zastoi* (stagnation) to Gorbachev's *perestroika,* a number of interesting shifts can be seen in other areas (see Figure 24).[5]

While *samizdat* was a key audience favorite in the Brezhnev years, singled out by 6 in 10 listeners, by 1986, when *perestroika* was underway and the Soviet press had begun to shake off some of the shackles of censorship, the rate had dropped in half. What formerly could only be expressed in *samizdat* form could, in the *glasnost'* period, often be openly debated in the Soviet press, thus denting part of the unique appeal of Western radio.

Political analysis and programs on life in the West remained important throughout Radio Liberty's history, but showed an increase in 1986. At this time, straight information was much more available in the USSR than hitherto, but there was often a lack of relevant analysis. Survey respondents throughout the *perestroika* period frequently noted that they now had access to information, but lacked competent analysis to place it in context and make sense of it.

Radio Liberty Program Preferences: 1975 and 1986

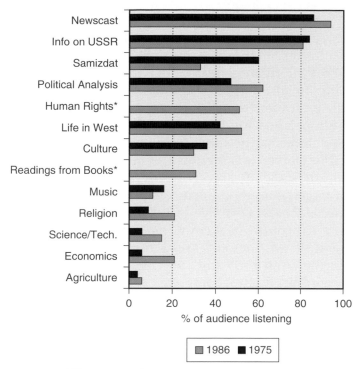

% of audience listening

■ 1986 ■ 1975

* These categories were not included in the 1975 survey questionnaire.

FIGURE 24. Listening to Different Types of Programming on Radio Liberty: 1975–1986

"Human Rights" and "Readings from Books" (usually books that originated in the USSR but were not allowed to be published there, such as works by Solzhenitsyn or Pasternak) were a continuing staple of Radio Liberty broadcast fare and resonated strongly with its "liberal" audience.

In the *perestroika* period, we also saw increasing interest in programs on religion, and in applied topics such as science and technology and economics. Now that reform was on the Soviet agenda, listeners sought out practical information on how to live in a society that was moving beyond traditional Marxist-Leninist ideological strictures. Radio Liberty's programming adapted to these new circumstances and evolved from a largely "dissident" perspective in the Brezhnev years to a more all-round focus on politics and information by 1986.

3.5. Listeners' Perceptions of Major Western Broadcasters

Data from the *perestroika* period show how listeners perceived the major broadcasters in terms of "relevance" to the listener, the "credibility" of the information heard, the relative friendliness or sharpness of the broadcast "tone," and assessments of the stations' overall "professionalism." Figures 25–28 provide net scores in these four areas for 1985 and 1987.[6] (Net scores are determined by subtracting negative from positive assessments.)

By 1987 Radio Liberty was seen as the most relevant of the Western broadcasters, slightly ahead of VOA (see Figure 25). This was no doubt largely due to its focus on current affairs in the USSR and especially to its coverage of *perestroika*. Radio Liberty was becoming a participant in the internal debate on reform in the Soviet Union. It was the only Western radio to increase its relevance rating between 1985 and 1987, while the Soviet press was growing more lively. By adding greater coverage of USSR affairs to its mandate to explain America to Soviet listeners, VOA managed to stay at much the same score. BBC and Deutsche Welle, while both scoring positively, trailed somewhat on relevance. Both stations had less on-air time than Radio Liberty, with its round-the-clock transmissions, and they were required to spend a proportion of their broadcast time covering British and

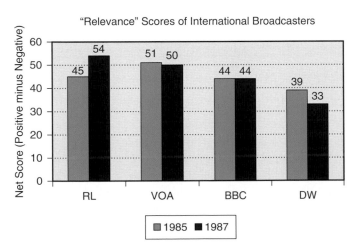

FIGURE 25. Trends in Perceived "Relevance" of International Broadcasters: 1985–1987

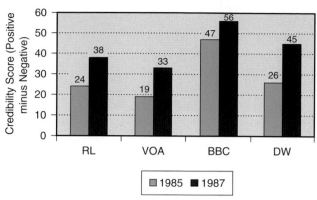

"Credibility" Scores of International Broadcasters

FIGURE 26. Trends in Perceived "Credibility" of International Broadcasters: 1985–1987

German affairs, both topics of secondary interest to the Soviet population.

In terms of relative credibility, however, BBC led the field (see Figure 26). With a net score of 56, it placed well ahead of Deutsche Welle, with Radio Liberty and VOA somewhat behind. Both Radio Liberty and VOA broadcasts at this time showed more political commitment than BBC and Deutsche Welle, and this may have influenced responses. While credibility *per se* was rated high for each station (53%), they were also cited for "tendentiousness" more frequently than either BBC or Deutsche Welle, thus lowering their overall net scores.

The way Radio Liberty's listeners assessed its tone was no doubt influenced by the station's forthright engagement on behalf of human rights, its extensive coverage of dissent in the USSR and its political edge. In 1985, many listeners felt its tone was critical rather than friendly. This assessment had changed by 1987 when it moved into a positive score, but Radio Liberty was still considered by its listeners to be more critical of the USSR than other international broadcasters.

BBC, known for its laconic broadcast style, scored highest on the tone scale, and this is probably related to its higher scores for credibility as well. Higher net scores across the board for all radios in 1987 may also be attributed to their adapting to the *perestroika* and *glasnost'* environments. Another factor may be that information that was coming out under *glasnost'* tended to

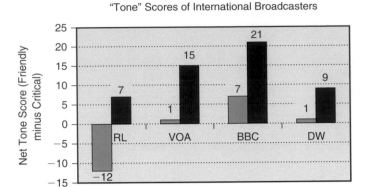

"Tone" Scores of International Broadcasters

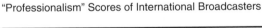

FIGURE 27. Trends in Perceived Broadcast "Tone" of International Broadcasters: 1985–1987

confirm much of what Western radio had been saying about events and conditions in the USSR.

All broadcasters scored relatively high in terms of all-round professionalism (see Figure 28). It's interesting to note that all net scores increased from 1985 to 1987. This may be related to their efforts to cover *perestroika* in the USSR, and the greater access they had to Soviet information sources by this time. In

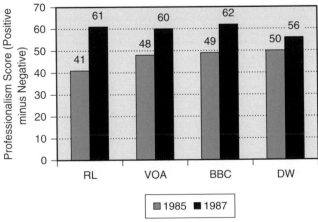

"Professionalism" Scores of International Broadcasters

FIGURE 28. Trends in Perceived Overall "Professionalism" of International Broadcasters: 1985–1987

any event, the professional quality of Western broadcasts in the Soviet media context was rated highly by listeners.

In sum, listeners changed their perceptions of Western broadcasters between 1985, when Gorbachev first came to power, and 1987, when *perestroika* and *glasnost'* were in full swing. This can probably be attributed to two factors: a) the capacity shown by Western stations to adapt their programming to the new environment in the USSR, and b) the audience's increasing interest in the unprecedented developments brought on by *glasnost'*.

SECTION

Western Radio's Place in the USSR Media Environment

4.1. Information Sources Used for National and International News

In 1981, the MIT computer simulation methodology was applied to data gathered during the late 1970s in order to ascertain how Soviet citizens received information on local, national and international topics.[1] The study was based on 4,496 interviews conducted with Soviet travelers from the urban parts of the USSR. A major aim of the analysis was to determine how Western radio fit into the larger media consumption patterns of Soviet citizens.

Figure 29 shows the main sources of national and international information in the urban USSR. Interestingly enough, the main source for local news (not shown here) was word-of-mouth (49%) followed by newspapers (49%), domestic radio (44%) and meetings (43%). Television, the most popular source for national and international news ranked only fifth for local information at 38%, suggesting that the rather centralized Soviet TV lagged in its coverage of local events.

Overall, TV led as an information source on both national and international events, but was followed closely by newspapers at the national level. Radio was in third place, followed by word-of-mouth[2] and *agitprop* meetings.[3] The importance of word-of-mouth communication at all three levels is symptomatic of an underlying skepticism toward domestic media sources. It correlates highly with Western radio, which was clearly a

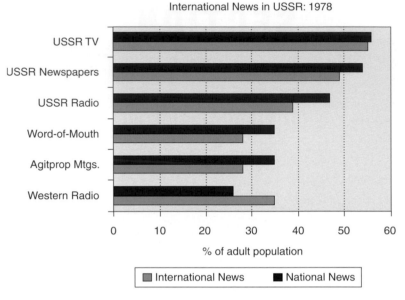

Main Sources of Information for National and
International News in USSR: 1978

% of adult population

■ International News   ■ National News

FIGURE 29. Sources of Information in the USSR for National and
International News: 1978 (Adult Urban Population)

player on the media scene, scoring 26% as an important source
for national news and 35% for international news.

Two inferences can be drawn from the media consumption
patterns shown here. First, rather than relying on a single
source of information, Soviet information-seekers preferred to
draw on a broad combination of sources. Secondly, the relatively low utilization of all official sources for information
(Soviet TV came in at only 55% and 56%), along with the
importance of face-to-face communication, and the fact that a
significant part of the population apparently did not seek
information at all, suggest that, for information purposes
at least, official Soviet media were failing to reach a substantial
segment of the population. The relative importance of Western
radio enhances the impression that official information channels were perceived as inadequate.

4.2. Media Use by Demographic Characteristics

Media consumption patterns varied according to age, gender,
education and Communist Party membership.

Age. Reliance on newspapers and domestic radio increased with age. Inversely, the use of Western radio and word-of-mouth diminished with age. Young people showed the least interest in TV and *agitprop* meetings, while the 30–49 year group showed the most. The media consumption patterns of the young indicated a mild "generation gap," corroborated by their attraction to more unconventional sources of information, such as Western radio. The over-fifties showed a higher reliance on newspapers and radio, and lower utilization of TV, meetings and personal contacts.

Education. Those with less than secondary education showed lower rates of use of all domestic information channels, although TV and newspapers ranked highest. In contrast, those with secondary or higher education ranked higher on all media with the exception of word-of-mouth. Respondents with higher education showed the highest rates of newspaper use and Western radio listening.

Gender. Women showed lower rates than men in all categories, although their scores were similar on word-of-mouth communication. Their scores on using Western radio for national or international information were less than half those of males.

Communist Party Membership. As a group, Communist Party (CPSU) members scored highest of all categories in their aggregate use of Soviet media for information. TV ranked first among them, with official meetings as the number two source. CPSU members ranked lowest of all the demographic groups on word-of-mouth communication, at a rate about half that of non-members. It's noteworthy that the scores for Western radio listening for Party members and non-members were essentially the same.[4] In other words, membership or non-membership of the CPSU was not an important predictor of Western radio listening. Party members were as likely as non-members to listen to Western radio for information on national and international topics. Given their need for accurate information and high level of interest in politics this is not surprising, although it does run counter to conventional stereotypes.

Geographic Regions. Geographically, newspapers scored highest in Leningrad, Moscow and the Baltic States, and lowest in Siberia, Central Asia and European Russia. Television was highest in Moscow and Leningrad, and lowest in Moldavia, the Trans-Caucasus and Central Asia. Radio followed a similar pattern. In terms of word-of-mouth communication, the Trans-Caucasus,

Leningrad, Moscow and the Baltic States scored highest. Aggregate use of media for information was highest in Moscow, Leningrad, the Baltic States and the Trans-Caucasus, with the lowest rates found in Central Asia, Siberia and Moldavia.

4.3. Media Use by "Factor Types"

In terms of national news, a factor analysis conducted on the sample defined three major types of media consumer: "independent-official," "orthodox-official" and "independent-critical."

- The "independent-official" group made use of all official media sources, but was more inclined to use Western radio than the average respondent. This group was dominated by men over thirty who were members of the the intelligentsia, but not the Communist Party.
- The "orthodox-official" group relied most heavily on the official domestic media channels. It was closely associated with middle-aged, male, white-collar members of the Communist Party.
- The "independent-critical" group used Western radio and word-of-mouth more extensively than the other types. Demographically, the "independent-critical" group differed from the "independent-official" group in that it was younger, included a larger proportion of Muscovites, and used official media sources less.

In terms of international news, two factors were generated, the "independent-critical" and the "orthodox-official" groups. Both groups were relatively well-informed, but the "orthodox" group, heavily influenced by CPSU membership, relied much more on official media sources, while the "critical" group depended much more on Western radio and word-of-mouth sources. Although the "orthodox" group showed scant predilection for word-of-mouth communication, they were still above-average users of Western radio. CPSU members were much less likely than non-members to discuss their Western radio listening with others.

In terms of individual stations, Radio Liberty and BBC showed the highest correlation with the "independent-critical" group. VOA and Deutsche Welle showed higher correlations with the "orthodox-official" group, although they also had links to the "independent-critical" group.

The fourth area, use of "unofficial" media sources—word-of-mouth and Western radio—wasn't covered in the Soviet source material but the SAAOR data tallied closely with other Western research in this area. A high positive correlation was found between Western radio use and word-of-mouth communication. As noted earlier, this link provided an amplifier effect for the messages contained in Western radio broadcasts, and indirectly increased their reach and impact throughout the Soviet population as a whole.

An additional behavioral pattern was noted which did not appear among the media consumption groups generated at either national or international information levels, but which clearly emerged from the correlation matrix used in the factor analysis. Word-of-mouth was the only information channel used to any extent among this residual group, and strong negative correlations were shown with other information sources. In other words, these people were "non-consumers" of official information. That is not to say that they weren't exposed to official media. That would be highly unlikely. What the data show is that they did not use the official media for *information*. This relatively uninformed and uninterested group appears to represent a substantial segment of the sample population. In effect they are information drop-outs, the equivalent of the "indifferent" group noted above in the attitudinal typology (see Figure 20).

The media study provided what was at the time an unprecedented opportunity to compare the results of SAAOR data with internal Soviet studies on media use[5] and to gain numerous insights on Soviet media consumption patterns. The findings lined up closely in the three main areas examined: general selection of media sources, demographic characteristics of users of different media, and typologies of media selection behavior.

The overall consistency between SAAOR data and internal USSR media studies increases our confidence in the reliability of SAAOR findings on the role of Western radio in the Soviet media context.

4.4. Trends in Media Use: 1978–1988

By 1988 *glasnost'* was the order of the day in USSR media, and it became apparent that Soviet citizens did not use media for information gathering in the same way they had done in the

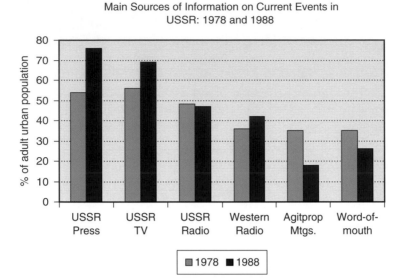

Main Sources of Information on Current Events in
USSR: 1978 and 1988

FIGURE 30. Main Sources of Information on Current Events in the USSR: 1978 and 1988 (Adult Urban Population)

late 1970s. Overall, Soviet domestic media were being used more as a source of information in 1988 than in the Brezhnev period. The press, which perhaps best reflected the new openness brought by *glasnost'*, had overtaken television, which remained under tighter state control (see Figure 30). Soviet citizens also appeared to have more confidence in their media than in pre-*glasnost'* days.

While use of domestic radio remained essentially steady at just under half the adult urban population, the use of Western radio increased slightly. In 1988 Radio Liberty was the only Western station still jammed. The drop in *agitprop* meetings and word-of-mouth in 1988 is noteworthy. *Glasnost'* was moving Soviet media usage patterns more in the direction of other modern industrial societies, where official propaganda methods carry less weight. The drop in word-of-mouth communication as an important source of information also reflected the growing freedom and credibility of the Soviet media under *glasnost'*. A high degree of reliance on word-of-mouth communication is a hallmark of authoritarian and totalitarian societies, where it is often viewed as more credible than official sources of information.[6]

SECTION

Western Radio and Topical Issues: Six Brief Case Studies

Examining the role played by Western radio and Radio Liberty in forming listeners' opinions on specific events can be instructive in helping to understand the stations' larger impact on their audience. Over the years, SAAOR placed a range of topical attitudinal questions in its traveler surveys. They allow us to take a close-up view of Western radio listening behavior in specific circumstances. Here we will briefly look at the fateful Soviet military involvement in Afghanistan, the *samizdat* phenomenon in the USSR, the downing of the Korean airliner, the Chernobyl nuclear disaster, *glasnost'* and *perestroika*, and the rise of Solidarity in Poland. Each case presents specific aspects of domestic media and Western radio use.

5.1. The War in Afghanistan: 1979–1989

SAAOR began gathering data on the attitudes of Soviet citizens to the war in Afghanistan in the early 1980s, and published its first findings on the subject in 1985.[1] In 1988, a trend report tracing the evolution of attitudes toward the war, and the role that Western radio played in informing Soviet listeners (based on 6,059 data cases), showed that disapproval of the war had risen from one-quarter of the population in 1984 to almost half in 1987, while those who held no opinion dropped from about half to one in three (see Figure 31).[2] Those who had been uncertain in their attitudes toward the war moved to disapproval, while

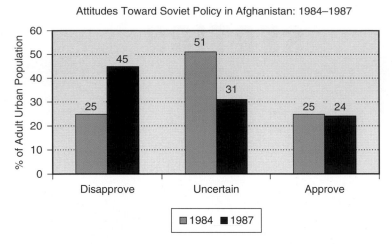

FIGURE 31. **Attitudes Toward Soviet Policy in Afghanistan Among Urban Adults: 1984–1987**

approval rates held steady. In the early years of the war, respondents tended either to minimize its importance and avoid expressing a viewpoint, or to recite stereotyped responses based on domestic Soviet propaganda. It was only after several years of involvement in Afghanistan that clearly-defined attitudes toward

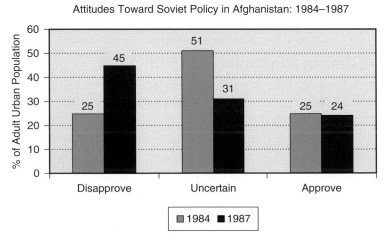

FIGURE 32. **Sources of Information on the War in Afghanistan Among the Soviet Adult Urban Population: 1984–1987**

the war began to be expressed by a majority of respondents in the traveler survey.

An analysis of information sources on Afghanistan show that Western radio played a significant role in informing the Soviet population about the war. Figure 32 shows that in 1987 ca. 45% of the urban population received information on the war from Western radio, compared with ca. 55% who cited the Soviet press and 50% who cited Soviet TV. Word-of-mouth was indicated by ca. 46% of respondents, roughly the same proportion who cited Western radio. As noted above, there is a high correlation between using Western radio and word-of-mouth as information sources.

Agitprop meetings were cited by ca. 38% of respondents in 1984, but this figure had dropped to 15% in 1987. It may be surmised that, by 1987, as the war began to go badly and the problems encountered began to receive attention in the Soviet press, *agitprop* lecturers were less inclined to confront critical audiences on this thorny topic.

When attitudes toward the war were correlated with information sources on the war, it became apparent that those who received their information from Western radio or via word-of-mouth communication were considerably more critical of Soviet policy than those who relied on official sources (see Figure 33).

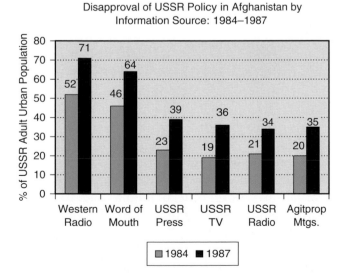

FIGURE 33. Disapproval of USSR Policy in Afghanistan by Information Source: 1984–1987

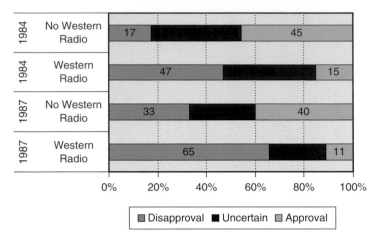

FIGURE 34. Attitudes to USSR Policy in Afghanistan Among Listeners and Non-Listeners to Western Radio: 1984–1987

While users of all information sources saw the war more negatively in 1987 than in 1984, the critical rate for Western radio listeners attained 71%, followed by 64% for word-of-mouth.

In 1984, Western radio listeners in general were roughly three times more critical of the war than non-listeners (see Figure 34).

In 1987, about two-thirds of Western radio listeners disapproved of the war and only about one in nine supported it. Clearly, information on the war supplied by Western radio played an important role in spreading anti-war sentiment among the Soviet population. It's also important to note the doubling of disapproval among non-listeners. Under *glasnost,'* critical coverage of the war began to appear in 1987 in the Soviet press.[3] Information from soldiers returning from Afghanistan was widespread throughout the population, and this, coupled with continuing coverage of the war by Western radio, created a situation where official media had to move beyond a narrow propaganda-based approach to the war if they were to maintain any credibility at all.

Criticism of the war had surfaced in the CPSU ranks by 1987, according to SAAOR data. In 1984 only 8% of party members disapproved of the war but this proportion had increased

Attitudes to USSR Policy in Afghanistan by
CPSU Membership: 1984–1987

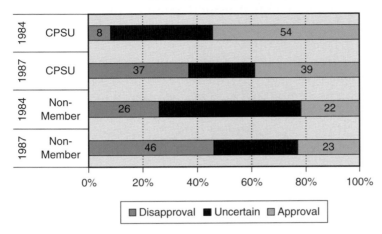

FIGURE 35. **Attitudes to USSR Policy in Afghanistan by CPSU Membership: 1984–1987**

to 37% by 1987 (see Figure 35). Support dropped from 54% in 1984 to 39% in 1987. When the Party rank and file began to lose faith in the war effort, the Afghan adventure was clearly doomed.

Secretary Gorbachev announced in February 1988 that the USSR would withdraw its military forces from Afghanistan, and the pull-out was completed a year later.

Data gathered by SAAOR in 1988 and 1989, after Gorbachev's announcement, indicated a high degree of disillusion with the Afghan adventure.[4] While 90% of respondents approved of the decision to withdraw, 69% of those queried felt that the USSR had failed to achieve its goals, and only 15% felt that it had achieved them. Fifty-nine percent of the respondents thought that the USSR's involvement in the Afghan conflict would have a lasting impact on Soviet society, while 29% felt that it would not. Among the effects cited were: diminished trust in the CPSU and the government, problems with veterans, and increased ethnic tensions. Sixty-eight percent of Western radio listeners felt that the war would have lasting effects, compared with 49% of the non-listeners. The listeners especially felt that trust in public institutions had decreased. Their sentiments were prescient for the future.

5.2. The *Samizdat* Phenomenon: 1970s

The *samizdat* phenomenon provided Western radio, and especially Radio Liberty, with one of its central programming themes in the 1970s. *Samizdat* (literally "self-published" materials) in some cases expressed political dissent, but also included literary works that failed to receive the official seal of approval, as well as information on human rights. *Samizdat* was an important part of the Soviet intellectual scene since the Sinyavsky-Daniel trial of 1966.[5] In the 1970s, it provided the democratic and human rights movements in the USSR with an essential means of expression to convey their message to the outside world, bypassing the narrow confines of small intellectual groups in a few large urban centers, where a limited number of typescripts passed from hand to hand. Western radio stations broadcast *samizdat* materials that reached the West back to the USSR, thus making them accessible to the larger Soviet population. *Samizdat* was a staple of Radio Liberty broadcast fare, but was also carried by VOA, BBC and some other Western broadcasters.

During the period March 1974 to March 1977, SAAOR gathered responses on a battery of questions concerning *samizdat* from 3,821 Soviet citizens traveling outside the country.[6] The MIT computer simulation methodology was used to project this data on to the adult population of the USSR.

According to the SAAOR study, slightly less than half the population of the USSR (44%) was aware of the *samizdat* phenomenon (see Figure 36). Of these, over half were aware from

Awareness of *Samizdat* in the USSR: 1977

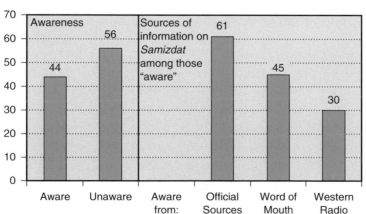

FIGURE 36. Awareness of *Samizdat* in the USSR: 1977

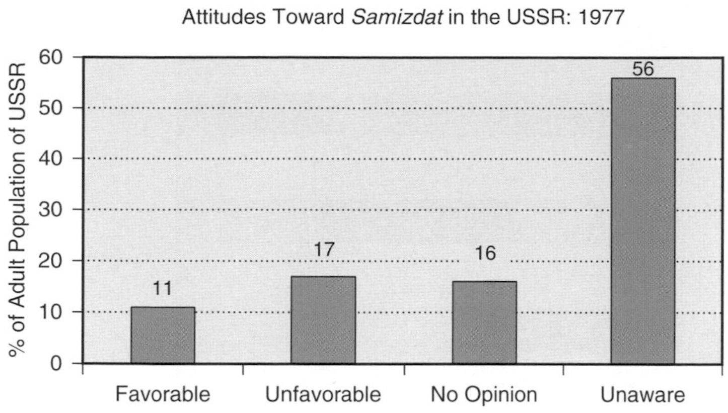

Attitudes Toward *Samizdat* in the USSR: 1977

FIGURE 37. Attitudes Toward *Samizdat* in the USSR: 1977

official sources, while about three in ten knew of *samizdat* from Western radio broadcasts. Word-of-mouth, not surprisingly, was also an important source, being noted by almost half of those aware of *samizdat*.

Only about one in nine Soviet citizens had a favorable opinion of *samizdat*. Among those aware of *samizdat*, about a quarter approved of it (see Figure 37). This finding was no doubt colored by the relatively high number of respondents who had heard about *samizdat* from official sources, which would have cast it at least in a negative light, at most as a treasonous activity. Once again, the "favorable" figure of one in nine comes close to the estimate of the proportion of "liberals" in the Soviet population already cited (see Figure 20).

Attitudes of Western radio listeners to *samizdat* put the phenomenon into a certain perspective (see Figure 38).

Radio Liberty listeners, already cited as the most "liberal" audience to Western radio, were in a large majority favorable to *samizdat* (about 7 in 10) while only 8% were negative. The favorable rating dropped to one in three for the composite audience to other Western radio stations (excluding Radio Liberty listeners). Among non-listeners to Western radio there was little sympathy for *samizdat*.

In the 1970s the *samizdat* phenomenon and the related human rights movement in the USSR was a major topic of Radio Liberty broadcasting. There is a strong correlation between listening to Radio Liberty and approval of this form of dissident activity, decried by a majority of the Soviet population.

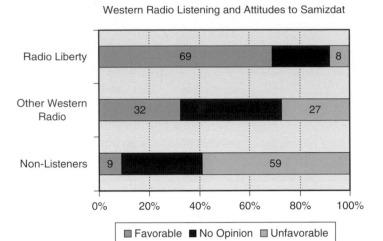

Western Radio Listening and Attitudes to Samizdat

FIGURE 38. **Western Radio Listening and Attitudes to** *Samizdat*

5.3. The Korean Airliner Incident: 1983

The Soviet downing of flight KAL 007 on September 1, 1983 provided a clear test of the efficacy of Western radio. The version of events communicated to Soviet listeners was almost diametrically opposed to that of official Soviet sources. In the two months immediately following the tragic incident, SAAOR, in the course of its normal survey program, queried 274 Soviet citizen travelers on their reactions to the incident and their sources of information on it.[7]

From the outset, Western broadcasters to the USSR gave heavy coverage to the KAL incident. Soviet media, however, during the first week of September, restricted their discussion of the affair to cryptic hints that a foreign plane had violated Soviet airspace. Not until September 7 did *Pravda* acknowledge that the Korean Airliner had been shot down by Soviet air defense. This signalled the launching of a full-scale media and *agitprop* campaign aimed at mobilizing domestic opinion in support of the government's position. In view of the sheer volume of commentary on the incident, it is not surprising that almost all respondents claimed to be aware of the event. In fact, 62% of them said they had heard about the KAL incident from *agitprop* meetings (see Figure 39). It's quite possible that many of the respondents had been briefed before traveling abroad so that

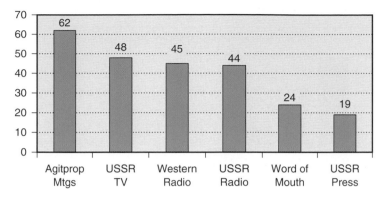

FIGURE 39. **Sources of Information on the KAL Incident**

they would know how to respond "correctly" to questions on the topic.

Western radio, mentioned by 45% of respondents, compared favorably with Soviet TV and domestic radio as an information source. However, a striking dichotomy in attitudes was found between those who had heard about the incident on Western radio and those who had only heard the official Soviet version. About eight in ten of the non-listeners to Western radio accepted the official Soviet version of events, while only 18% of the Western radio listeners found the Soviet version credible (see Figure 40). Over half the Western radio listeners believed the version of the incident they had heard on the broadcasts, while another 30% were uncertain which version to believe. The relatively large percentage of "don't knows" among the Western radio listeners may stem from the fact that they had been exposed to two conflicting versions of the incident and found it difficult to reach a conclusion. But their readiness to express uncertainty indicated a reluctance to accept the official version in the face of contradictory information.

The attitudes expressed by respondents to the Soviet action are consistent with the version of the incident to which they had been exposed, and which they had found more credible. (See Figure 41).

70% of the non-listeners approved the Soviet action in downing the Korean aircraft while only 22% of the Western radio listeners did so. Conversely, almost half the listeners

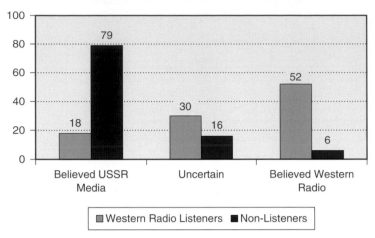

FIGURE 40. Credibility of Media Sources on KAL Incident Among Listeners and Non-Listeners to Western Radio

disapproved of the Soviet action and another third were unsure.

While the sample size in this spot survey was relatively small, the dichotomy that emerged between listeners and non-listeners was instructive. Some skepticism of the Soviet

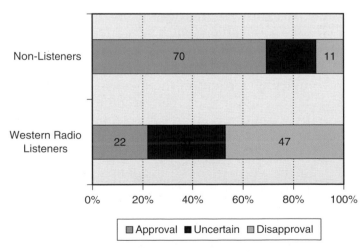

FIGURE 41. Attitudes Toward the USSR Action in the KAL Incident Among Listeners and Non-Listeners to Western Radio

version of events may well have existed without Western radio information sources. But it is questionable that an 'alternative opinion' could have been formed. For this, outside information was necessary. It's interesting to note that, in the first week or so after the downing of the aircraft, most respondents showed a good deal of confusion over the matter. At that stage, their natural response was to voice support of their government. Only after enough time had passed to allow the Western radio version of events to be repeated in a consistent manner, while the Soviet version emerged in a halting, and at times contradictory, form, were clear opinion changes noticed.

5.4. The Chernobyl Disaster: 1986

In the two months immediately following the Chernobyl disaster on April 26, 1986, SAAOR put queries about the incident to 528 Soviet citizens in the course of its regular surveys.[8] This study provided an unusually good opportunity to assess the impact of Western radio broadcasts because of the inept manner in which the catastrophe was handled in Soviet media.

Soviet media did not report the accident at the Chernobyl nuclear power plant on the day it took place, but waited until two days after the disaster occurred. In the ensuing weeks, some information, often contradictory, trickled out from official Soviet sources, but no complete account was given to the Soviet population. (Soviet officials eventually gave a sober account of the accident to a meeting of the International Atomic Energy Agency in August 1986.)

In this information vacuum, many Soviet citizens sought out other information sources for an account of what happened. The first source of information on the tragedy among SAAOR respondents was Western radio, indicated by 36% (see Figure 42). This was followed by Soviet TV at 28% and word-of-mouth at 15%.

Even after Soviet media began to report on the accident, Soviet citizens continued to turn to Western radio for further information. An additional 13% used Western radio as a supplementary source after first hearing about the disaster from USSR media, making a total of 49% of the survey group to turn to Western

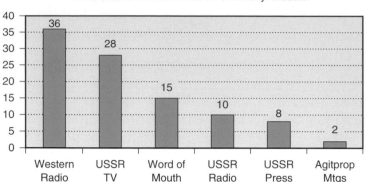

FIGURE 42. **First Source of Information on the Chernobyl Disaster**

radio. VOA was cited most frequently among Western radios as a first source of information on Chernobyl (18%), followed by Radio Liberty at 8% and BBC at 7%. In all, 28% of the respondents had heard information about Chernobyl from VOA, 18% from Radio Liberty and 16% from BBC.

When Soviet media was either slow or unforthcoming in reporting on a major issue, Western radio often filled the gap, as the case of Chernobyl clearly demonstrates.

5.5. *Glasnost'* and *Perestroika:* 1985–1990

The impact of *glasnost'* on Western radio listening has already been noted. Listeners to Western radio had different priorities from non-listeners in the area of reform and consequently had a somewhat different perspective on the government's approach to *perestroika* and its chances of success.[9] Although both listeners and non-listeners felt that the need for economic reform was the USSR's most pressing problem (32% and 28% respectively), listeners were far more concerned than non-listeners that the problems were rooted in the very nature of the Soviet system itself (24% versus 10%).[10] It might be inferred that the detailed analyses of *perestroika* carried on Western radio may have been a factor in prompting listeners to seek the roots of the problems in the system, while non-listeners gave higher priority to more immediate goals such as higher living standards and security issues.

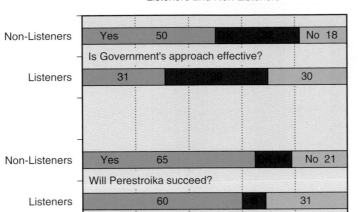

Evaluation of Perestroika by Western Radio
Listeners and Non-Listeners

FIGURE 43. Evaluation of Gorbachev's Approach to *Perestroika* and Its Chances of Success by Listeners and Non-Listeners to Western Radio[11]

With a different perspective on events, Western radio listeners were considerably more skeptical of the government's approach to reform. Whereas half of the non-listeners felt that the government's handling of *perestroika* was effective, only three in ten Western radio listeners shared this view (and another 30% contradicted it). A majority of both listeners and non-listeners felt that *perestroika* would eventually succeed, but here again listeners were more skeptical, with ca. three in ten convinced it would be less than successful.

By and large, Western radio broadcasts were favorable to the concept of *perestroika* and reform in the USSR. But their coverage of the process was more critical than that of Soviet media, and this appeared to resonate with its listeners who supported reform, but were concerned that *perestroika* had more to do with words than with concrete deeds.

5.6. The Solidarity Movement in Poland: 1980–1981

The Solidarity labor movement in Poland was a complex issue for Western radio to explain to their Soviet listeners. The development of attitudes among SAAOR respondents over three time periods in 1980–1982 is shown in Figure 44.[12]

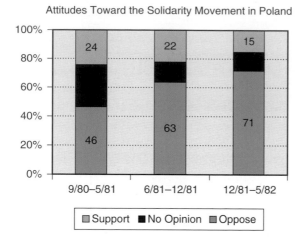

Attitudes Toward the Solidarity Movement in Poland

FIGURE 44. **Trend in Attitudes Toward the Solidarity Movement in Poland: 1980–1982**

In 1980, as the situation in Poland was heating up, opinions were already fairly negative, with almost half opposing the activities of Solidarity. This increased to almost two-thirds between June and December 1981, as the situation grew increasingly tense. After the imposition of martial law in December 1981, and during the following months, opposition grew to 71%, with only 15% expressing support of Solidarity. Again, this corresponds roughly to the proportion of "liberals" in the urban USSR shown earlier in Figure 20.

During the first year of the Polish developments, Western radio listeners showed more inclination to support liberalization in Poland than non-listeners (by 26% to 14%). Radio Liberty listeners were more favorably inclined than others (42%), a finding which is doubtless linked to the more critical (or more "liberal") orientation of the Radio Liberty audience. These general tendencies continued into the post-martial law period, although Western radio listeners were not immune to the rise in anti-Solidarity feeling. Most striking of all was the finding that, during the martial law period, virtually none of the non-listeners to Western radio were favorable to Polish liberalization (3%).

Although a high correlation has been shown between "liberal" attitudes and Western radio listening, the data in this case suggest that Western information on Poland failed to strike a responsive chord outside any but the most critically-oriented stratum of Soviet society, and that even there it most likely did little more than reinforce previously held viewpoints. Official Soviet information on Poland seems to have successfully mobilized opposition to Solidarity around three major themes which appealed to the emotions and perceived self-interest of Soviet citizens: the danger of strikes, portrayed as a counter-revolutionary activity leading to social breakdown or chaos; the latent mistrust of Poles shared by much of the Slavic population of the USSR; and the perceived threat to national security. The lesson to emerge from this case study is that Western radio was less able than domestic media to influence the Soviet population when the direct interests of the average Soviet citizen were made to appear threatened.

SECTION

Some Observations on the Impact of Western Broadcasting to the USSR

An assessment of the overall impact of Western radio in the USSR during the Cold War must remain incomplete in the absence of conclusive evidence from the Soviet archives, which given current restrictions on such data is not apt to be forthcoming in the near future. (However, the paper given at the conference on Cold War Broadcasting Impact at the Hoover Institution in October 2004 based on internal Soviet data from the late 1970s- early 1980s by Dr. Elena Bashkirova, a former researcher at the Institute of Sociology of the USSR academy of Sciences confirms the findings of large audiences to Western broadcasts and some comparisons with SAAOR findings are made in the epilogue section of this study.) But there is ample empirical evidence to support the view that Western radio broadcasts played an important role in helping to inform the Soviet public, and preparing them to go beyond Marxism-Leninism. Four points in particular stand out:

1. Western radio drew surprisingly large audiences in the USSR during the Cold War, as has now been confirmed from both internal and external sources;

2. Western broadcasts were clearly important in the eyes of the Soviet regime. The broadcasts were widely attacked in Soviet media, and the regime attempted to discourage listeners by means of jamming and intimidation, even to the extent of laying down criminal penalties for spreading information heard on Western broadcasts;

3. Western broadcasters, by their presence and popularity, played a significant role in forcing Soviet domestic media to reform and modernize;

4. Information from Western broadcasts played a crucial role in helping to form or reinforce democratic attitudes in the USSR.

6.1. Large Cold-War Audiences

As this paper has demonstrated, Western radio had sizeable audiences during the Cold War period, with at least 30–40% of the adult population being reached at one time or another. There are few examples of external information sources managing to reach into a modern, industrialized society in such a broad and consistent fashion. The sheer size of the audience to Western broadcasts in the USSR bears witness to the need felt by many members of the Soviet population to go beyond their official domestic media to satisfy their need for information.

6.2. Widespread Regime Attacks

Soviet domestic media, especially the press, constantly published articles (which may have numbered well in the thousands) attacking and criticizing Western radio broadcasts. As well as possibly discouraging listening among some, these media attacks may well have had the unintended effect of publicizing Western radio and thereby increasing curiosity about its programming. This is a topic that is beyond the scope of this study and will be treated in a separate analysis.

6.3. Effect on USSR Media

Western radio shattered the information monopoly to which the Soviet regime aspired. There is widespread evidence that the competition posed by Western radio was one of a number of factors that spurred Soviet media to undertake reform on several occasions, to avoid being sidelined as a source of information by their home audience. Additionally, by depriving Soviet media of an information monopoly, the presence of Western radio influenced the ways in which Soviet media would cover a story, forcing them in many instances to stay closer to the facts.

According to the American researcher Dr. Maury Lisann, writing in 1975, Soviet media were even then feeling pressure from Western broadcasts:[1]

"The Soviets began serious investigation of basic public attitudes and audience reactions around 1965 and in connection with that explicitly cited problems presented by the existence of foreign broadcasting. The salient facts of those investigations, insofar as the limited raw data that were disclosed can be interpreted are as follows. About 40 to 60 million people, with varying degrees of regularity, listen to foreign radio broadcasts. Major questions of public interest that are known mainly through foreign radio coverage reach and are of interest to 50 to 75 percent of various population groups. From 30 to 50 percent of the population consider the response of Soviet broadcasting to be inadequate. In addition, from 20 to 30 percent of the population, and perhaps more, seem generally to doubt the credibility of all Soviet information sources, and by inference, much of the basic ideological legitimacy of the system."

Lisann's estimates of audience size, though based on fragmentary data gleaned from Soviet publications, are largely borne out by the SAAOR findings.

Since at least the 1960s, it had been clear to some members of the USSR leadership that Soviet media would have to adapt in order to meet the information challenge posed by Western broadcasters. An article in the official Soviet journal *"Kommunist"* of July 1965 sounded the alarm:[2]

"Bourgeois propagandists are trying to use foreign radio, press, tourism, as channels of penetration of alien views in our midst. It would be rash on our part to be satisfied that these channels have not justified all the long-range hopes of the anti-Soviet propagandists. It is necessary to study the tactics of enemy propaganda and actively counteract them. . . ."

This was followed by a spate of press articles exhorting Soviet media to improve news coverage and generally make their programs more attractive. The domestic radio station Mayak, founded in 1964, was broadly organized along a Western broadcasting model that combined a new emphasis on news with attractive musical programming, and was seen as a domestic alternative to foreign broadcasts.[3] (It was also used to jam these same broadcasts.)

A new media magazine, RT (*Radio I Televidenie*) was created in 1966 to rebut information contained in Western radio broadcasts. The *Vremya* TV news program went on the air on January 1, 1968 with a new, modern approach to news and current events. The ability of Soviet citizens to find alternative sources of information unquestionably put pressure on Soviet media to improve their performance with regard to the quality and timeliness of the information provided, and the format in which it was presented.

The impetus to improve and adapt Soviet media to compete more effectively with foreign broadcasts continued into the *glasnost'* period. In 1987, major innovations were made in Soviet television.[4] Programming became more timely, interesting and attractive. By bringing television news and information up to the level of Western radio broadcasts (now widely available to Soviet citizens, since most were no longer jammed), the regime clearly hoped to make domestic television a more valuable tool in the service of the state.

6.4. Influence on Attitude and Opinion Formation

The examples cited in Section Five, though episodic, make it clear that Western radio, by providing information unavailable from domestic sources, played an important role in the complex process of shaping Soviet listeners' opinions on events. High positive correlations, however, are not proof of causality.

Obviously, the process of opinion formation does not depend on any one single factor. It is entirely possible that, during the pre-*glasnost'* period, Western broadcasts did little more than reinforce already existing critical positions among the approximately one in eight Soviet urban adults who were highly critical of the Soviet system, and whom we have typified as "liberals." Nevertheless, the broadcasts served as an informational lifeline which ensured that the existing critical standpoint could be nourished and consolidated.

For the 30% of the urban adult population who were characterized in the attitudinal typology as "moderates," Western radio provided alternative and supplementary information without which a critical thought process might have been inconceivable. It was when the "moderates" and the "liberals" found common ground in the *perestroika* period that change became possible.

Although Western radio was in communication with the more critically-thinking elements in Soviet society, its audience was not limited to these groups. It was widely heard among the elites of Soviet society, including members of the CPSU, who listened at approximately the same rates as non-members. They tuned in not only to "know the enemy," but also to obtain the information they needed to function effectively in leadership roles in their own society. Over time, their understanding of events and processes at work in the USSR was inevitably colored by the information and analysis they received from Western broadcasts.

Although Western radio was less effective in reaching the politically apathetic, the less-educated party members, and ideological hardliners, these groups were never part of the audiences the radios were aiming for, which was, broadly speaking, the urban intelligentsia. None of these groups, moreover, played a significant role in the transformational process of the late *perestroika* period.

6.5. Summing Up

Western broadcasters did not have a blueprint for the democratic development of the Soviet Union but, by keeping hope of change alive, and by maintaining a dialogue with those elements of the population that were working for, or at least open to, change, they made an essential contribution to the eventual transformation of the USSR.

International radio communication alone is not enough to bring about basic changes in a society, though it is difficult to imagine that a freer and more pluralistic society could have evolved in the Soviet Union without the contribution of Western radio. But the broadcasts were a means, not an end. They were a channel of information that reported the news, but they didn't make the news. They helped to keep the flame of hope alive, but there had to be a vessel to contain that flame.

That vessel was the large audience that was receptive to these broadcasts, to the factual information they provided and the implicit message of hope they contained. This was a committed audience that strained to listen through jamming or found ingenious methods to circumvent it. The Soviet peoples themselves, in association with a somewhat and sometimes enlightened leadership in the *perestroika* period, saw the necessity for change and transformation, and eventually made it possible to put an end to the Cold War and begin a new chapter in their lives. Western radio played an indispensable part in the process, but in the end real change came from within, not from without.

This is an empirical study based upon available quantitative data, and it is easy to forget that there is a real human being with his or her personal story behind each number. This rather straightforward presentation of statistics and correlations doesn't do justice to the emotions that listeners expressed in thousands of letters to the stations over the years, or in off-the-cuff comments during interviews. That would be a worthwhile topic to explore but it's for another study. In closing, perhaps an Institute Director in Kiev expressed best what Western radio meant to her, and to many like her, in a letter to Radio Liberty in 1989:

> "In my opinion, and I speak for a circle of Ukrainian intellectuals in Kiev, we feel that all the changes taking place in the USSR today are in great part due to Western radio broadcasting the truth. Especially Radio Liberty because it devotes so much time to events in the USSR. If the radio stopped broadcasting, we would feel betrayed . . . it would be a disaster."

SECTION

EPILOGUE. Comparison of SAAOR Findings with Data from the Archives of the Institute of Sociology of the USSR Academy of Sciences: Late 1970s and Early 1980s.

As noted above, a comparison with work from the Soviet archives is now possible based on the paper given by Dr. Elena Bashkirova at the October 2004 conference on the impact of Cold War Broadcasting held at the Hoover Institution.[1] Dr. Bashkirova was a researcher at the Institute of Sociology of the USSR Academy of Sciences (referred to as ISAN below) and based her paper on research carried out by the Institute of Sociology in the late 1970s through the early 1980s. Although the methodology was obviously different from that employed by SAAOR, the Soviet research confirms large audiences to Western radio broadcasts during the period and allows for comparisons in a number of areas.

The data cited by Dr. Bashkirova is based on 6,365 respondent cases selected on the basis of proportional quota sampling in 6 major Soviet cities. These were considered by the Institute of Sociology researchers to be approximately representative of the urban population of the USSR. No national surveys were undertaken. The reasons cited for this were 1) to avoid attracting attention that would be inevitable for a nation-wide study, and 2) the researchers hypothesized that the audience to Western radio in the provinces and rural areas was probably too small to be of significant interest.[2]

7.1. Comparative Listening Rates

Overall weekly listening rates in the ISAN study and SAAOR data for the period are very close (see Figure 45), with the ISAN rate of 27% only slightly higher than the SAAOR rates.[3]

The ISAN study also noted a very high rate of occasional listening (less than once a week) to Western broadcasts, i.e. 35% of the urban population. Combined, these two figures showed that "by the end of the 1970s more than half of the USSR urban population listened to foreign broadcasting more or less regularly."[4] This overall reach estimate of 62% is considerably higher than the annual reach of 34% tallied by SAAOR in 1980. One of the reasons that the ISAN rates are higher may be due to the fact that they are based on an urban sample only, while the SAAOR rates are based on simulated national samples. Another reason is likely the large number of "accidental" listeners and young people listening for entertainment who were much less likely to be captured in the traveler sample to which SAAOR was restricted.

7.2. Demographic Comparisons

In demographic terms, the SAAOR and ISAN samples are consistent in terms of education trends: listening increases in each as educational levels increase. ISAN noted that those with secondary

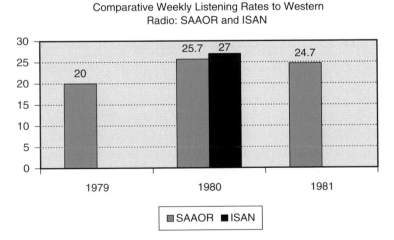

Comparative Weekly Listening Rates to Western Radio: SAAOR and ISAN

FIGURE 45. Comparative Weekly Listening Rates to Western Radio: SAAOR and ISAN, 1979–1981

or higher education "composed about 70% of the total western radio audience."[5] In 1980 ca. 74% of Radio Liberty's audience fell into this education category. The estimate for all Western radio listeners would have been slightly lower as Radio Liberty's audience was characterized by a relatively high educational level. A difference in the two datasets is noted in the case of age. Young people aged 16–24 listened at the highest rates and made up 44% of the audience to Western radio in the ISAN sample. In 1980, the year that corresponds closely to the ISAN sample, Radio Liberty's audience also had its highest rate of listening among young people aged 16–29, although this situation shifted during the remainder of the 1980s and highest listening rates were then noted in the 30–49 year age cohort (see Figure 17).

In terms of listening in different parts of the USSR, the two datasets identify similar patterns. SAAOR identified highest listening rates to Western radio in the Moscow and Leningrad areas and in the Baltic States and Trans-Caucasus. The ISAN data also noted that "in the regions close to the state borders of the USSR the interest in Western radio programs was somewhat higher than in the central parts of the country. The Baltic Republics, Western Ukraine and Caucasian Republics of the former USSR are especially noteworthy in this connection."[6]

7.3. Motivations for Listening, Programs Heard and Trust in Western Information

As indicated above, the ISAN surveys identified music and entertainment as a motive for listening to Western broadcasts at much higher rates than did the SAAOR data (ca. 69% in the ISAN data compared to only ca. 20% in the SAAOR data). We hypothesize that this is largely due to the difference in samples. ISAN was able to survey a representative number of young people while SAAOR had to rely on a much smaller group of younger travelers who may have been largely atypical of their age cohort in terms of their interest in news and information and the outside world.

However, in going beyond this atypical group we find that many of the other reasons given for listening to Western radio line up quite well between the two datasets. About 45% of the ISAN sample sought news and information and 38% listened to have a better understanding of the situation in the USSR. These are the reasons most frequently cited by the SAAOR traveler survey as well (see Figure 23). Bashkirova states: "The audience interest in the information programs of Western radio was high, because the listeners could get information about international events which were not covered by the Soviet mass media due to various reasons."[7]

In detailing respondents' motives for listening to Western radio, after the high proportion singling out music and entertainment, the ISAN data indicates that 33% were "searching for information that differs from the official point of view," 27% were looking for "exclusive information," another 20% sought "hot news," 20% were "interested in information unavailable in the Soviet mass media" and another 7% said they were "searching for trustworthy information."[8] All of these categories imply that listeners were seeking something that they couldn't find in Soviet domestic media. Since some of the respondents obviously indicated more than one of these categories we can't simply add them together (that would total 107%!), but it's apparent that a very large proportion of listeners had strong information-seeking motives in tuning to Western broadcasts. This finding is entirely consistent with SAAOR data.

In terms of trust in what Soviet respondents were hearing from Western radios, Bashkirova, in her study of the ISAN data, notes: " . . . the Soviet social scientists were suspicious about the finding that the Western broadcasting was so popular with the Soviet population, which found it both trustworthy and reliable."[9] The ISAN data indicates that 37% trusted the information either completely or partially, 32% said they didn't trust the data and 31% didn't venture an opinion. Bashkirova notes "overall, the level of trust in the information broadcast by Western radio was sufficiently high when one considers that the figures include non-listeners as well as listeners." When one considers that some respondents may have been reluctant to admit in a Soviet survey that they trusted information from "enemy" sources these figures are impressive, indeed, with more respondents saying they trusted the information rather than disbelieving it.

These findings on trust cannot be compared directly to SAAOR data of the exact time period, since the question was not asked then, but a similar pattern emerges in looking at SAAOR data from 1985 and 1987. Net "credibility" scores (the percentage finding the broadcasts credible minus the percentage who did not) showed that all major stations had positive "credibility" scores (see Figure 26), meaning that more listeners trusted what they heard than didn't.

Given the high number of people these percentages represent, it's apparent from both the ISAN and the SAAOR data that millions of Soviet listeners were tuning to Western radio for news and information on a regular basis and to a greater or lesser extent believing what they heard.

7.4. Western Stations Heard

The ISAN data was primarily aimed at studying the audience to Western radio in general in terms of its behavior, motivations and social structure and didn't attempt to compute weekly and overall reach figures for individual stations. Consequently, no comparisons between the two datasets can be made at that level. ISAN did, however, ask in a general sense what stations people heard and here the rank ordering of stations is very similar between the two datasets for 1979–1980, with VOA in first place in both, followed by BBC in second with Radio Liberty and Deutsche Welle lower (see Figure 1 and Figure 2 for SAAOR estimates).

7.5. Conclusions

A comparison of the ISAN data and the SAAOR data from the same period show striking similarities.

- Overall regular listening rates are similar in the two datasets, although because of the nature of the differing samples the ISAN data was able to capture a larger group of occasional listeners and young people who listened to entertainment programs.
- Demographic trends are consistent with the exception of the young group noted above due to sampling differences.
- Both datasets show that large numbers of Soviet citizens sought Western radio broadcasts as alternative sources of information.
- Trust in the information broadcast on Western radio was relatively high in both samples.

APPENDIX

SAAOR Survey Methodology: Interviewing Soviet Travelers

Shortly after going on the air in 1953, Radio Liberty began to gather empirical evidence of listening habits in the USSR under the direction of Dr. Max Ralis, the first Director of Audience Research. The first major interviewing effort took place at the Brussels World Fair in 1958. Over 300 Soviet citizens were contacted, of whom 65 turned out to be listeners to Radio Liberty (even more heard VOA and BBC). Interviewing of Soviet travelers continued through the 1960s on an *ad hoc* basis. Though considerable evidence on listening habits was gathered, it was impossible to undertake any statistical analysis of the findings and project them back to the Soviet population.

From 1970 onwards, with greater numbers of Soviet travelers in the West in the period of "détente," SAAOR began to systematize its data collection methods. Interviews were entrusted to independent survey research institutes, and a standard questionnaire was developed. However, because of reluctance on the part of many Soviet travelers to submit to a classic open interview, the institutes working for SAAOR did not find it practical to apply directly an open structured questionnaire in the interview meeting. Rather, the interview was conducted as part of a general discussion on media with the respondent. The interviewer filled out the questionnaire immediately after the conclusion of the discussion. To remove the possibility of any built-in bias, the interview did not focus solely on any single Western radio station but dealt with the broader subject of

Western broadcasting to the USSR. Interviewers were unaware of a special interest on the part of any specific Western station. In fact, the data was shared with all major Western broadcasters to the Soviet Union: VOA, BBC, Deutsche Welle, Radio Canada International and Radio Sweden International all benefited from the research.

The problems involved in interviewing Soviet travelers to the West in the 1970s and early 1980s did not arise when interviewing visiting Eastern Europeans (RFE's East European Audience and Opinion Research unit was separate from SAAOR until September 1990. It carried out an extensive program of interviewing East European travelers). Soviet travelers generally found themselves under some form of group control and could be apprehensive in dealing with non-Soviets. There was evidence that many groups had been given special briefings on how to deal with people they might meet in the West. Additionally, Soviet travelers, especially in the earlier years, were a selective (and "selected") group, less representative of the population as a whole than their Eastern European counterparts.

Receiving permission to travel abroad was difficult and usually involved a screening process for loyalty to the regime. However, the traveling population did include a wide representation from among those groups that Western radios were most interested in reaching, namely urban, educated adults. There was a considerable bias toward members of the Communist Party with about a quarter of the travelers interviewed being Party members, against only 9% of the adult population.

Strict verification of the survey work was carried out at two levels. First, local institutes were responsible for the on-going verification of all data collection by carrying out random spot-checks to ensure that interviews were actually taking place. Careful procedures were developed for this purpose. Additionally, SAAOR field specialists regularly monitored the output of the institutes and conducted numerous on-the-spot checks to ensure the integrity of the data. Secondly, from the late 1970s on, a method of Comparative and Continuous Sampling, originally developed by Dr. Henry O. Hart, Director of Radio Free Europe's Audience and Public Opinion Research Department, was employed. The computerized data were carefully analyzed for internal consistency between sampling points before being accepted for use in analysis. Chi-square tests were applied to sub-sets of the data being gathered in different areas, and if results did not show statistical consistency, the data would not be used for analysis. The purpose was to ensure that travelers to each sampling point belonged, so to speak, to the same "universe," and that local differences in interviewing conditions did not substantially impact the findings. Dr. Hart's method represented a major breakthrough that made it possible to use survey techniques on traveling populations to study the behavior of non-traveling populations.[1]

As the traveling population increased in the mid-1980s and became both less supervised and less apprehensive in their contacts with non-Soviets, it became possible to use the questionnaire in the interview meeting. The questionnaire at this point was modified to take advantage of recent technology, and became computer-readable to facilitate rapid processing of the data. In the late 1980s, over 5,000 interviews were taking place each year and provided a rich and unique database for the study of media behavior and attitudinal patterns in the USSR. By the time surveying of travelers ended in mid-1990, SAAOR had built up a database of over 50,000 structured interviews covering the period 1972–1990.

By the late *perestroika* period in 1989, SAAOR was able to move beyond the study of public attitudes on *ad hoc* issues to examine the latent structure of Soviet public opinion. Working with a French institute, Agorametrie, which had developed sophisticated models for studying public opinion structures in Western Europe, SAAOR fielded a supplementary questionnaire that provided data to map the Soviet population along several attitudinal dimensions. This permitted a more sophisticated understanding of the positioning of Western broadcasters, in terms of attitudinal types in the population, media use, and views on a range of topics of the day. This was a major advance from SAAOR's first attempt to develop an attitudinal typology of the Soviet population in the 1970s.

This work on the analysis of the structures of public opinion and the role of media and Western radio led in 1991–1993 to a strategic cooperation with a leading international research firm based in France and Switzerland, the International Research Institute on Social Change (RISC). By this time SAAOR had become the Media and Opinion Research Institute (MOR) of the

RFE/RL Research Institute in Munich. Together, MOR and RISC joined in surveys and analysis to study the processes of social change in the former Soviet Union and Eastern Europe during the post-Communist transition period. Furthermore, in collaboration with Central European Market Research (CEM), and Prof. Jan Jerschina of Cracow University in Poland, MOR developed the PSE Expert model, which was also applied to the post-Communist transition processes. Since the PSE model focused particularly on the political dimension, it complemented the RISC study which emphasized the socio-cultural dimension. The findings of both will be analyzed in a later study.

To sum up, SAAOR interviewing of Soviet travelers to the West evolved from modest ad hoc beginnings in the 1950s and 1960s, to a systematized but still somewhat unorthodox approach in the 1970s, to a standardized survey approach in the 1980s. From gathering individual accounts of listening in the early days, it advanced to providing a database for estimating audiences for Western radio in the USSR, and finally to placing these Western radio messages in the context of a broader understanding of communication processes and attitudinal structures within the Soviet Union.

APPENDIX

The MIT Mass Media Computer Simulation Methodology

The MIT computer simulation methodology was developed under contract from the United States Information Agency to study the sociology of Soviet audiences for mass communications. The MIT team was headed by Dr. Ithiel de Sola Pool, Professor of Political Science at MIT. Its findings were published in a series of reports in 1975, all of which are noted in the select bibliography to this paper. The input data for this initial study came from SAAOR interviews conducted in 1970–1972. Professor Pool gives a detailed account of the methodology used in this first simulation application in the methodological report issued as "Simulation Report 4" in the report series.

The MIT simulation methodology is described in some detail in an article in *Communications Research: An International Quarterly* of October 1982. The article was authored by Professor Pool, Dr. John Klensin, Principal Research Scientist at MIT and R. Eugene Parta, Director of SAAOR. An earlier, detailed example of the application of the simulation methodology was included in "Listening to Radio Liberty in the USSR, 1976–77," Analysis report 3-78, SAAOR, by R. Eugene Parta. Those wishing more details on the methodology are referred to the above publications as space limitations here do not permit more than a highly simplified general description.

The simulation methodology was developed to address the basic issue of how to draw estimates from uneven samples, given that the sample deficiencies could not be corrected in the field.

After applying extensive cross-checks to ensure that the data were internally consistent, the next step was how to estimate underlying data from aggregated results, in this case estimating individual cell values in a contingency table (which in some instances might be quite weak or even missing) from the table's marginals (which would be considerably more robust). The algorithm for this computational process was dubbed "Mostellerization." It had been developed by Prof. Frederick Mosteller of Harvard University (see select bibliography) and was first applied in the simulation process to create a population model of the USSR. The table was based on input from Soviet census data, but the data were not available in a multi-dimensional format that could be used by the simulation. It was necessary to create a new 4-way demographic table (age by education by gender by rural/urban residence) from lower dimension tables in the census data. This provided a 24-cell table with 3 levels of age, 2 of education, 2 of gender and 2 of rural/urban residence. The next step was to create a 240-cell table by factoring in ten geographic regions. The final step in creating the population model was to expand it to 480 cells by factoring in Communist Party membership, data which was not included in the census but had to be found elsewhere—in this case, in *Partinaya Zhizn'* ("Party Life").

Since samples were insufficient to compute listener estimates in all 480 cells of the population model directly, the second stage of the simulation relied on the Mostellerization algorithm to make estimates of underlying cell data from aggregated listener-ship figures. This procedure followed the same process as above, but substituted listening ratios for population figures to compute first the 48-cell table, and then expand this to 480 cells to take into account geographic dispersion. The ratings calculated in each cell, multiplied by the population model values for the cell, provided the basic estimate of the audience.

As normal confidence interval tests could not be applied, a special algorithm was developed that provided estimates of cell reliability on a cell-by-cell basis. Estimates of cell reliability are largely dependent on the sample size collected for that cell, and more importantly, the degree to which that cell needed to be weighted relative to other cells. These reliability estimates were made by assessing the impact, on a cell-by-cell basis, that mis-classification of a single respondent would have on the audience estimate. This means that listening tallied in a cell with a low sample population but a high real-world population (e.g., old, uneducated, rural women) would result in a low sense of confidence about that cell. In estimating a confidence range for an entire table this cell would have a strong impact. Conversely, this procedure gives more confidence in cells where the sample population is large and considerable listening is recorded (e.g., educated, middle-aged urban males). In terms of final estimates the direction of bias in the raw sample data coincided with those strata of the population most likely to engage in Western radio listening, the activity being measured. The result is a relatively strong sample in the cells that contribute most heavily to the listening estimates.

In 1986 the "core audience" concept was introduced. This derived estimates precisely from that part of the sample which was most robust and where most listening to Western radio occurred—the urban, educated, adult population—which made up about a quarter of the entire adult population. This permitted listening trends to be charted more accurately than using the entire adult population where confidence ranges were considerably larger.

In the 1980s, the simulation methodology was adapted more specifically to SAAOR's particular needs. When it was determined that Communist Party membership was not a predictor of listening to Western radio, this dimension could be collapsed out of the simulation process, yielding two basic input tables: a 24-cell demographic table (age, sex, education, rural/urban) and a 20-cell geographic table (geographic region by education) which was "mostellerized" into a final 240-cell output table.

Two MIT methodologists deeply committed to the 1980s effort to refine the MIT simulation process for SAAOR purposes were Dr. John Klensin, Principal Research Scientist at MIT and Dr. Ree Dawson, a Harvard-trained statistician. In 1986 Dr. Dawson wrote a paper "Developing a Methodology for Projecting the Audience to Foreign Broadcasts in the Soviet Union" (see select bibliography for details), which proposed a survey-ratio estimator model to build on the MIT simulation process for purposes of analyzing trends in listening. This was applied to the analysis of listening trends through the end of the project in 1990. In 1988 Dr. Dawson developed a log-linear method for imputing sample values for SAAOR estimates of geographic audiences (see reference in select bibliography) which permitted the geographic estimates to be calibrated more precisely than hitherto. These are the estimates used in the 1988–1989 charts provided in this paper.

The MIT simulation process could be applied to other purposes than estimating audiences to Western radios. When sample sizes were sufficient, SAAOR used the procedure to study the *samizdat* phenomenon in the USSR, and to study overall media consumption patterns, as reported above in this paper.

SAAOR acknowledges its deep debt to Prof. Ithiel de Sola Pool and his MIT colleagues in developing and applying a pioneering statistical methodology that made possible a deeper understanding of the role and impact of Western broadcasting to the USSR during the Cold War.

APPENDIX

Data Validation:
Comparison of SAAOR Studies with
Internal Soviet Studies and Other Data

Given the serious constraints on carrying out survey research on the USSR, and the lack of access to reliable Soviet data from the same time period, it was a complex task to assess the validity of the SAAOR data. Even under normal polling circumstances, different surveys can yield different results depending on specific question wording or sampling design. (This became evident when many of the surveys conducted in 1991–1992 by internal institutes frequently showed quite different results from one institute to the next.)

The novel research approach that circumstances constrained SAAOR to adopt significantly compounded these issues. However, it was occasionally possible to compare SAAOR findings with work done inside the USSR both during the Cold War period and immediately thereafter, and it is instructive to examine the correlations that emerge.[1]

C.1. Comparison of Findings from Separate SAAOR Data Bases (Emigrant and Traveler Surveys)

As noted earlier, SAAOR systematically interviewed Jewish emigrants from the USSR as part of a separate project entirely distinct from the travelers surveys. Since emigrants were a special group within the overall population, it was not SAAOR practice to use them to project listening rates to Western radio back on to the Soviet population. However, in many ways they were typical of non-emigrants in the same educational, age and geographic categories. Because of this, they constituted a useful surrogate group to study listening behavior in greater detail than with Soviet citizens. The emigrants' patterns of listening behavior were similar to those of respondents in the traveler surveys, although they listened to Western radio at much higher rates.

Emigrants listened to Western radio at twice the rate of travelers. This is not surprising, since they were, on average, more educated than the traveler population, and since emigration in the Soviet Union amounted to a political act. Figure 46, which is based on Western radio listeners in each sample, shows that station choice was consistent between the two samples, with an identical rank order and comparable rates.

In 1990, Radio Liberty was the station most widely heard among Western radio listeners in each sample, followed by VOA, BBC and Deutsche Welle. In the 1970s and 1980s, VOA was the most widely heard station, according to both emigrant and traveler surveys. The fact that two different "samples" yielded highly similar results, increases our confidence in the reliability of the data from SAAOR traveler surveys.

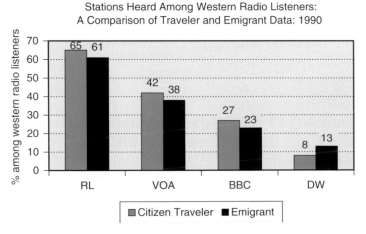

FIGURE 46. **Stations Heard Among Western Radio Listeners: A Comparison of USSR Traveler and Emigrant Data: 1990**

C.2. Comparison of Findings on TV Viewing Behavior (SAAOR Survey and Internal USSR Studies)

The first real opportunity to compare SAAOR data on Soviet media behavior with data from an internal study came in 1975. Data from a survey group of 1,832 respondents interviewed between 1972 and 1974 was compared in terms of demographic categories[2] with a study conducted in Leningrad a few years earlier.[3] While neither study attempted to project all-Union behavior (the SAAOR study was primarily interested in looking at the relationship between TV viewing and Western radio listening) the similarity of the results by demographic group is striking. Both studies show the same trend in terms of average hours of weekly TV viewing by educational attainment, with lower levels of TV viewing noted at higher educational levels (see Figure 47).

Similar results are noted for weekly hours of TV viewing by age (see Figure 48). The amount of TV viewing grew in each study with increasing age. Respondents over 40 years of age viewed considerably more television in an average week than did those under thirty.

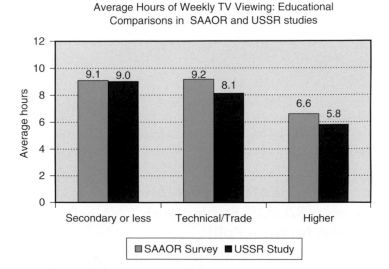

FIGURE 47. **Average Hours of Weekly TV Viewing by Education in SAAOR and USSR Studies**

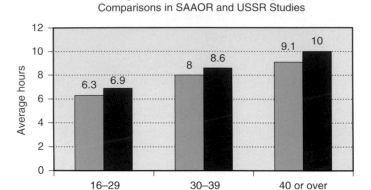

FIGURE 48. Average Hours of Weekly TV Viewing: Age Comparisons in SAAOR and USSR Studies

In terms of preferred programming, we again note a striking similarity between the two studies (see Figure 49). News and movies lead in each study. Only with economic programming, which was viewed by the lowest number in each study, is there a clear difference. Respondents in the SAAOR survey were more likely to choose programs on economic themes than respondents in the USSR study. This may be due to the higher educational level of the SAAOR traveler respondent sample. In each sample, however, this category ranked last.

It was noted earlier in this paper that the extensive media study based on SAAOR data in 1981 lined up closely with findings on media use from a variety of internal USSR sources.[4] The similarity of the findings in the specific comparative studies on TV behavior again help to increase our confidence in the SAAOR data as reliably depicting media usage patterns in the USSR.

C.3. Comparison of Attitudes to Andrei Sakharov (SAAOR Survey and Unofficial Internal Poll)[5]

During the Cold War period it was possible to compare SAAOR data not just with official studies, but also with unofficial polls conducted inside the USSR by Soviet social scientists, presumably of a "dissident" political bent.[6] The unofficial poll cited here was

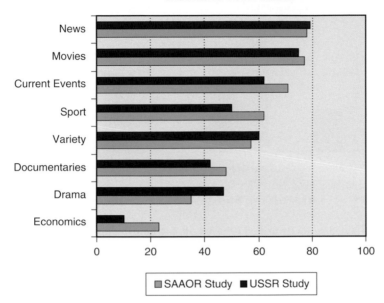

Types of TV Programs Watched: SAAOR
and Internal USSR Studies

FIGURE 49. **TV Program Preferences in SAAOR and USSR Studies**

based on 853 structured conversations with Soviet citizens in Moscow and surrounding areas in 1981. While it was not based on a scientific sample, the authors stated that considerable care was taken to reach a broad segment of the population.

The attitudes toward Sakharov that emerged from the unofficial poll were strikingly close to those found in a previously published SAAOR study.[7] About half the respondents in each study held no opinion of Sakharov, while those that did divided roughly three to two against him (see Figure 50).

While two polls, each employing an unorthodox methodology, cannot in scientific terms validate each other, it is instructive that the results from similarly gathered datasets should give such close results.

C.4. Comparison of Attitudes Toward Solidarity in Poland (SAAOR Survey and Internal Poll)

Another comparison with an unofficial internal poll concerned attitudes toward the Solidarity labor movement in Poland. The general findings of the SAAOR study have been presented

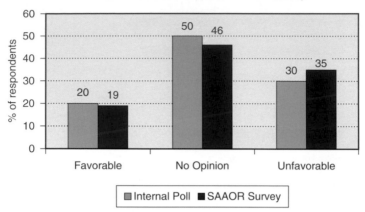

FIGURE 50. **Attitudes to Andrei Sakharov in an Unofficial Internal USSR Poll and an SAAOR Survey–1981**

above (see Figure 43). The Soviet poll was carried out at the same time as the SAAOR poll (September 1980–December 1981) with 618 respondents in Moscow and environs.[8] The survey methodology was similar to that used in the unofficial poll on Sakharov, i.e., a structured informal conversation in

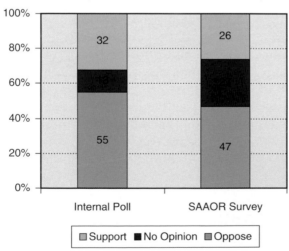

FIGURE 51. **A Comparison of an Unofficial Internal USSR Poll and SAAOR Survey Data on Attitudes Toward Solidarity in Poland**

which the questions were placed casually. The Soviet researchers noted that their respondent group was biased in favor of workers, intellectuals and CPSU members.

In each case, around half of those polled opposed Solidarity, while around three in ten supported it (see Figure 51). The responses of blue collar workers were virtually identical for the two groups, varying by only one percentage point. About one-fifth of the workers supported Solidarity and a third were undecided.

Again, unorthodox methodologies cannot scientifically validate each other but the similarity of the findings strongly suggests that a reasonably accurate picture of attitudes toward Solidarity was being sketched in the SAAOR data.

C.5. Comparison of Attitudes to *Perestroika* (SAAOR Data and Polls Commissioned in the USSR by Western Media Organizations: 1988–1989.)[9]

In the later *perestroika* period (1988), a few Western media organizations managed to include their own questions in internal Soviet public opinion studies. The French publications *Le Point* and *Le Matin*, as well as *Time* magazine and CBS-*New York Times*, worked on such studies with the Moscow-based Institute of Sociological Research. In areas where it was possible to make comparisons with SAAOR data, the French-sponsored studies were consistent with SAAOR findings on *perestroika*, withdrawal from Afghanistan, emigration from the USSR, and awareness of Andrei Sakharov and his work.[10]

Time magazine conducted a study in Moscow in March 1989 with the Institute of Sociology at the Academy of Sciences.[11] Some of the questions could be compared with results from SAAOR survey data and they showed similar results.[12] In the SAAOR poll, 34% felt that limits to *glasnost'* were undesirable, while in the *Time* poll 33% felt that there was not enough *glasnost'*. Support for Gorbachev was 78% in the SAAOR data and 79% in the *Time* poll. Sixty-eight percent felt that East-West relations had recently improved in the SAAOR data, while 63% held that view in the *Time* poll.

A CBS-*New York Times* poll in 1988 also queried Muscovites on their attitudes toward *perestroika*. SAAOR posed similar questions

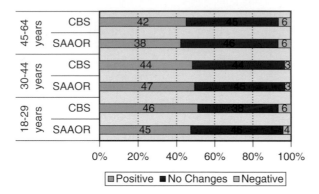

Comparison of SAAOR and CBS Internal USSR
Poll on Benefits of *Perestroika*

FIGURE 52. Comparison of CBS-New York Times Internal USSR Poll with
SAAOR Survey on Benefits of *Perestroika:* 1988

in its traveler surveys at about the same time. The comparative
results of the two polls, when examined in terms of age categories, are very close, as can be seen in Figure 52.[13] The two polls
showed approximately equal levels of support (or "no change")
in each category. Negative responses were very small in each
poll. Additionally, the CBS-*New York Times* poll queried respondents on how well they felt the USSR had succeeded in its policy
in Afghanistan. Twenty-five percent in the CBS-*New York Times*
poll felt that Soviet policy had completely succeeded. At that
point in early 1988, 27% in the SAAOR poll shared this opti-
mistic view (as noted above, this figure declined a year later in
1989). On the other hand, 33% in the CBS-*New York Times* poll
felt that Soviet policy had failed in Afghanistan compared with
37% in the SAAOR poll. Again, the results of the external and
internal polls are very similar.

C.6. Comparison of Findings on Western Radio Listening (SAAOR Survey and Internal Polls)

In 1990, it was possible to compare data on Western radio listening from the SAAOR traveler survey, which was in the field
for about the first six months of the year, with surveys conducted inside the USSR. The comparison was not exact in terms
of question wording and sample design, but proved nevertheless

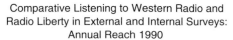

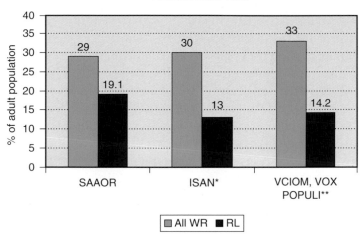

Comparative Listening to Western Radio and
Radio Liberty in External and Internal Surveys:
Annual Reach 1990

'ISAN Survey: Moscow, Leningrad, Kiev, Gus-Khrustalny
**VCIOM Survey: All-Union for Annual Reach: Vox Populi Survey RSFSR only

FIGURE 53. **Comparative Listening to Western Radio in External and Internal Surveys: SAAOR, Institute of Sociology of the USSR Academy of Sciences and VCIOM/Vox Populi: Annual Reach 1990**

instructive (see Figure 53). The SAAOR survey data represented the entire USSR. The ISAN (Institute of Sociology at the USSR Academy of Sciences) poll sampled three large urban centers (Moscow, Leningrad and Kiev) and a regional small city (Gus-Khrustalny). The VCIOM (All-Union Center for Public Opinion Research) had a representative sample of the entire USSR, and the *Vox Populi* survey covered the Russian Federation (RSFSR). The VCIOM survey provided a figure for aggregate listening to Western radio only, while the *Vox Populi* survey gave estimates only for individual stations. Their results are shown here side by side.

Both internal surveys showed slightly higher rates of listening to any Western radio in the past year than did the SAAOR data, although the results are within the same approximate range. Annual listening rates for Radio Liberty are somewhat higher in the SAAOR survey, but both internal surveys show high annual rates of listening to Radio Liberty as well. In sum, all three surveys present a relatively consistent picture of listening to Western radio and Radio Liberty in the USSR in 1990, the first year it was possible for Western organizations to commission Soviet research institutes to gather data on Western radio listening.

One of SAAOR's concerns in 1990 was that Radio Liberty might still suffer from the pariah status it had been assigned by Soviet media, and that this might lead to a problem of response bias in internally conducted surveys, with respondents hesitant to admit to Radio Liberty listening in a face-to-face survey conducted by the same interviewing networks that had formerly conducted government-sponsored surveys. Some anecdotal evidence surfaced to support this concern, but it was difficult to determine whether response bias effectively played a role in depressing Radio Liberty listening estimates. Since the results shown above were close to SAAOR estimates for the same period, this may be immaterial.

The results of a survey in St. Petersburg (ex-Leningrad) in 1991 can be compared with the SAAOR data from 1989 shown above (see Figure 12). The internal survey, conducted by the St. Petersburg Center for the Study and Forecasting of Social Processes found that Radio Liberty was heard by 20% of the population.[14] This compares with an estimated listening audience of 24% in Leningrad in the 1989 SAAOR data. While these numbers are not identical (the two-year gap in the survey dates should also be borne in mind), they both testify to similarly sized audiences in Leningrad/St. Petersburg.

Internal surveys conducted in the Baltic States in 1990 were compared with SAAOR estimates from 1989.[15] Average figures from the three internal surveys (two in Estonia and one in Lithuania) gave a weekly reach figure of 30% for Western radio listening overall, and 14% for RFE/RL.[16] SAAOR estimates for 1989 were 29% for any Western radio, and 18.6% for RFE/RL. Again, these estimates are all in the same approximate range, and all show a considerable audience to RFE/RL.

Finally, a similar pattern emerged from a comparison of SAAOR data with a Soviet-sponsored survey of audiences to Western radio in Lithuania. A poll commissioned by the newspaper *Sovetskaya Litva* studied listening habits among students in Vilnius. The Soviet survey reported that 50% of the students surveyed were Western radio listeners, while SAAOR's figure for this age group was 52%. Twenty-eight percent of the students in the Soviet poll heard RFE/RL, compared with 29% in the SAAOR data.

While these similarities in research findings are not scientific proof of the accuracy of the SAAOR data, they increase confidence that the findings are reasonable and that they do not run counter to other empirical evidence of listening.

In all the areas where comparisons could be made between internal studies and SAAOR traveler surveys, the results were close and the trends identical. This congruence of findings, while not scientific proof of the validity of the SAAOR traveler surveys, cannot be satisfactorily explained by either coincidence or good fortune alone, and is compelling evidence that the SAAOR methodological approach yielded reasonable and credible findings, both on Western radio and general media use and on public attitudes in the USSR.

ENDNOTES

Preface

1. The survey was carried out by Vox Populi on 11–12 September 1991 with a sample size of 1,000. Thirty-nine percent of the respondents said they listened to foreign radio broadcasts during the crisis: 30% heard Radio Liberty, 18% BBC, 15% VOA and 7% Deutsche Welle. The results were published in "Crisis Compendium: Analyses of Media Use in the USSR During the Coup Attempt," Report #1017/92, January 1992, Media and Opinion Research, RFE/RL Research Institute. Other studies carried out by local research institutes in the USSR published in this compendium showed high rates of listening to Radio Liberty's Russian service during the coup: Kiev 24%, Tbilisi 18%, Tallin 17%, Riga 38%, Yerevan 30%, Lithuania 35%. Listening was also high for broadcasts in the local languages (Ukrainian, Georgian, Estonian, Latvian, Armenian and Lithuanian) but generally lower than in Russian.
2. Based on a telephone survey of 704 members of Moscow-based political and intellectual elites carried out by Vox Populi between September 15 and 23, 1991. The report, Research Memorandum 1010/91 is published in the "Crisis Compendium" cited above.
3. "Yeltsin's Vital Radio Link With the Russian People," Leslie Colitt in the *Financial Times* of August 22, 1991.
4. See "Report from Moscow: An Eyewitness View of Soviet Putsch," Iain Elliot in the August-September 1991 edition of "Shortwaves," the RFE/RL in-house organ.
5. "How Radio Liberty Informed the Soviet Population," Dirk Schütz in *Die Zeit,* August 30, 1991.

6. "An Imprisoned Gorbachev Tuned into the World via Radio" by Thomas B. Rosenstiel in the *Los Angeles Times* of August 23, 1991.
7. The decree was printed in both the original Russian and in English translation in the August-September 1991 issue of "Shortwaves."

Section One: Measuring the Audience to Western Broadcasters in the USSR

1. For a short history of how this interviewing effort developed see R. Eugene Parta. "Soviet Area Audience and Opinion Research (SAAOR) at Radio Free Europe/Radio Liberty, in *Western Broadcasting Over the Iron Curtain*, K. R. M. Short, ed. Croom Helm, London/Sidney, 1986, pp. 227–244.
2. Audience Research at Radio Liberty was founded in 1954 by Dr. Max Ralis who continued in this position until his retirement in 1981. He was succeeded as Director by R. Eugene Parta, who had been working with Ralis since 1969. Dr. Ralis, who came to Radio Liberty from Cornell University, was a pioneer in developing a wide range of techniques, both qualitative and quantitative to study Soviet audiences to Western broadcasts. Audience research was located at RFE/RL headquarters in Munich until 1970 when it moved to Paris. It was known as Audience Research and Program Evaluation until 1981 when it took the name Soviet Area Audience and Opinion Research (SAAOR).
3. For details on the MIT simulation methodology as well as for more details on the interviewing procedure used in the 1970s see R. E. Parta, J. C. Klensin, I. S. Pool: "The Short-wave Audience in the USSR: Methods for Improving the Estimates," *Communications Research*, Vol. 9, No. 4, October 1982, pp. 581–606. Interviewing methods in the 1980s took on a more formal aspect.

Section Two: Trends in Listening to Western Broadcasters in the USSR: 1970–1991

1. See Dr. Ithiel de Sola Pool, Massachusetts Institute of Technology. "Soviet Audiences for Foreign Radio." USIA R-17–76, September 1976. With summary prepared by the Office of Research, United States Information Agency.
2. Ibid., p ii.
3. R. Eugene Parta, John C. Klensin, Ithiel de Sola Pool: "The Shortwave Audience in the USSR," op. cit, p. 603.

4. See R. Eugene Parta, "Weekly Audience Estimates for Major Western Broadcasters to the USSR: January 1973-June 1980," AR 10–80, Soviet Area Audience and Opinion Research, RFE/RL, Inc. December 1980. This report added separate estimates for the "urban population" as well for the four major broadcasters.

5. Michael Nelson, *War of the Black Heavens. The Battles of Western Broadcasting in the Cold War*. Brassey's, London, 1997. p. 20.

6. Ibid., Nelson, p. 116.

7. Rimantus Pleykis, *Radiotsentsura*. An article based on the author's earlier (1998) book, *Jamming*. The article contains updated material from 1998–2000 from information in Soviet archives. "Radio Baltic Waves," Vilnius, Lithania, May 2002. p. 6 and p. 37. Pleikys notes that stations were placed in 3 categories according to their perceived hostility: The first category included Radio Liberty, Kol Israel, Radio Tirana and Radio Peking. They were jammed round-the-clock with special noise-producing jamming transmitters. The second category included BBC, Deutsche Welle and VOA which were jammed by signals from the Soviet musical station "Mayak," which was not as effective as the noise-producing jammers. The third category included Radio Sweden, Radio Canada, Radio France International, Yugoslavia, Egypt, etc. which were not jammed at all after 1968. Radio France International never reported being jammed.

8. A favorite method to enhance audibility under conditions of jamming was to add the 16 and 19 meter bands to Soviet sets which generally did not include meter bands below 25 meters. Audibility was often better on these bands. The "twilight immunity" effect also meant that at certain times of the day jamming was considerably less effective than at other times. In urban areas "dacha listening" in the countryside was a favorite way to escape the heavier ground wave jamming in the cities.

9. Nelson, op. cit., p. 95.

10. Mark Rhodes, "Effects of Jamming on Listening Behavior," RM 10–85, Soviet Area Audience and Opinion Research, RFE/RL, Inc. October 1985.

11. Dawn Plumb, "Has the Nuclear Threat Increased? Some Soviet Citizens' Views," AR 1–84, Soviet Area Audience and Opinion Research, RFE/RL, Inc., February 1984. The data showed an increasing trend from July-September 1982 when 47% replied yes to the title question to October-December 1983 when 65% answered in the affirmative. 43% of the 2,983 Soviet citizens queried ascribed this to an "aggressive Western policy." Western radio listeners and non-listeners were of the same opinion that the nuclear threat had increased: 56% in each case.

12. Mark Rhodes and Amy Corning, "Radio Liberty Attracts Many New Listeners in 1989," RM 1–90, Soviet Area Audience and Opinion Research, RFE/RL, Inc. March 1990.

13. SAAOR Staff, *"Glasnost'* and the Soviet Media Environment: Implications for Western Radio," AR 1–88, Soviet Area Audience and Opinion Research, RFE/RL, Inc. March 1988.

14. Sallie Wise, "Soviet Citizens on Glasnost': High Expectations, Limited Impact." AR 5–87, Soviet Area Audience and Opinion Research, RFE/RL, Inc. December 1987. p. 16.

15. Mark Rhodes, "Glasnost' Has Not Diminished Importance of Foreign Radio," Research Memorandum 2–89, Soviet Area Audience and Opinion Research, RFE/RL, Inc. July 1989, p. 2.

16. See AR 2–87, R. Eugene Parta, "Trend Analysis 1986. Listening to RFE/RL and other Foreign Stations Among Core Audiences in the USSR." and AR 1–90, R. Eugene Parta, "Trend Analysis July-December 1989. Listening to RFE/RL and Other Western Stations in the USSR." Soviet Area Audience and Opinion Research, RFE/RL, Inc.

17. R. Eugene Parta and Ree Dawson, "Revised Geographic Listening Estimates to Foreign Radio in the USSR: Introduction of Log-liner Imputation Techniques for Geographic Estimates," AR 2–90, June 1990. Soviet Area Audience and Opinion Research, RFE/RL, Inc.

18. Ibid., pp. 5–14.

19. In 1988–1989 Radio Liberty broadcast to the USSR in Armenian, Azerbaijani, Belorussian, Georgian, Kazakh, Kyrgyz, Russian, Tajik, Tatar-Bashkir, Turkmen, Ukrainian and Uzbek. Additionally RFE broadcast in Estonian, Latvian and Lithuanian. VOA broadcast in Armenian, Azerbaijani, Estonian, Georgian, Latvian, Lithuanian, Russian, Ukrainian and Uzbek. BBC broadcast only in Russian. Deutsche Welle broadcast in Russian and Ukrainian.

20. For the sake of convenience, only those four major broadcasters which had the largest audiences are being included here. Of course, there were many other international broadcasters to the USSR, among them Radio France International, Radio Canada International, Radio Sweden, Radio Vatican, etc. but their audiences were generally smaller and because of this difficult to deal with in the MIT simulation.

21. The Moscow-based independent research institute ROMIR conducted the surveys during the period 1993–2001. They were published in RFE/RL's Media and Opinion Research Report series in 1993 and 1994 and thereafter by InterMedia Research Institute, the successor organization to MOR.

Section Three: Who Were the Listeners and What Did They Hear?

1. Here the Soviet Census definitions for rural and urban are used. "Urban" areas may go down to settlements as small as a few thousand people.

2. R. Eugene Parta, "Civil Liberties and the Soviet Citizen: Attitudinal Types and Western Radio Listening," AR 6–84, Soviet Area Audience and Opinion Research, RFE/RL, Inc. This was SAAOR's first attempt at putting together a typology of the Soviet population in order to better understand the position of Western radio listeners in the larger society. The analysis was based on a factor analysis of the data that isolated five questions (from a total of 14 that had been used during the survey period) that correlated highly on the issue of civil liberties to build an attitudinal scale which was then projected onto the urban population of the USSR using the MIT computer simulation methodology. The questions dealt with attitudes about issues such as freedom of speech, dissent, legality, the right to emigrate and racial tolerance. The methodology is explained in greater detail on pp. 16–29 of the report. Later, more sophisticated work, in looking at attitudinal patterns and types in USSR and later Russian society involved the application of the Agorametrie perceptual mapping methodology, the RISC segmentation (International Research Institute on Social Change) and the PSE Expert model, developed with Prof. Jan Jerschina of Cracow University and Central European Market Research. This work will be examined in a subsequent study.

3. Mark Rhodes, "Perceptions of Western Radio: How Soviet Citizens View Radio Liberty, VOA, BBC and Deutsche Welle." AR 3–85, Soviet Area Audience and Opinion Research, RFE/RL, Inc.

4. Mark Rhodes and Patricia Leroy. AR 4–87, "Comparative Audience Perceptions of Major Western Broadcasters to the USSR," Soviet Area Audience and Opinion Research, RFE/RL, Inc.

5. Data for this chart are taken from AR 3–78, R. Eugene Parta, "Listening to Radio Liberty in the USSR: 1976–77" and AR 3–87 Mark Rhodes, "Patterns of Listening to the Russian Service of RL," Soviet Area Audience and Opinion Research, RFE/RL, Inc.

6. Data for these charts are taken from AR 3–85. "Perceptions of Western radio: How Soviet Citizens View RL, VOA, BBC and DW" and AR 4–87, "Comparative Audience Perceptions of Major Western Broadcasters to the USSR: January 1985—June 1987," Soviet Area Audience and Opinion Research, RFE/RL, Inc.

Section Four: Western Radio's Place in the USSR Media Environment

1. R. Eugene Parta and Mark Rhodes, "Information Sources and the Soviet Citizen: Domestic Media and Western Radio," AR 5–81, Soviet Area Audience and Opinion Research, RFE/RL, Inc. This study carries an extensive section on comparisons of the SAAOR data with Soviet studies on media behavior, showing that they come to essentially the same findings, with the exception of Western radio listening, data on which was not published in the Soviet studies.

2. In analyzing communication in totalitarian societies, Prof. Ithiel de Sola Pool states that reliance on word-of-mouth " . . . reflects a massive lack of confidence in the national media . . .," and that "foreign radio listening is a second choice for use when credible domestic sources are lacking." See "Communication in Totalitarian Societies," in *Handbook of Communication,* Ithiel de Sola Pool and Wilbur Schramm, eds., Rand McNally, New York, 1974, p. 470.

3. *Agitprop* comes from "agitatsiya and propaganda" and in this context refers to the structured organization of meetings, briefings and lectures held in local Party organizations, at the workplace and in other public venues. This was a highly developed system in the USSR and served as a channel for the Party to get its views and positions across to its membership and to the larger population.

4. Parta and Rhodes, "Information Sources . . .," op. cit., p. 7. The scores for Party members for Western radio listening were 59 vs. 61 for non-members. These scores are the totals of use of Western radio for national and international news.

5. Ibid., pp. 21–27.

6. See Pool, Schramm, pp. 470–471.

Section Five: Western Radio and Topical Issues: Six Brief Case Studies

1. Sallie Wise, "The Soviet Public and the War in Afghanistan: Perceptions, Prognoses, Information Sources," AR 4–84, Soviet Area Audience and Opinion Research, RFE/RL, Inc.

2. Sallie Wise, "The Soviet Public and the War in Afghanistan: Discontent Reaches Critical Levels," AR 4–88, Soviet Area Audience and Opinion Research, RFE/RL, Inc.

3. Ibid., pp. 12–13.

4. Sallie Wise, "January 1989 Data on the Aftermath of the Afghan War," Internal SAAOR Memorandum, February 23, 1989.

5. See Peter Reddaway, *Uncensored Russia: Protest and Dissent in the Soviet Union*, American Heritage Press, New York 1972.
6. R. Eugene Parta, "Samizdat, The Soviet Public and Western Radio." AR 9–77, Soviet Area Audience and Opinion Research, RFE/RL, Inc.
7. R. Eugene Parta and Kathleen Mihalisko, "The Korean Airliner Incident: Western Radio and Soviet Perceptions," AR 4–84.
8. Sallie Wise and Patricia Leroy, "The Chernobyl Disaster: Sources of Information and Reactions," AR 4–86. Soviet Area Audience and Opinion Research, RFE/RL, Inc.
9. Sallie Wise, "Soviet Citizens on Glasnost: High Expectations, Limited Impact," AR 5–87, Soviet Area Audience and Opinion Research, RFE/RL, Inc.
10. Sallie Wise, "Soviet Citizens on Gorbachev's Domestic Policies: Continuing Support But Growing Skepticism," AR 5–88, October 1988, Soviet Area Audience and Opinion Research, RFE/RL, Inc.
11. Ibid.
12. R. Eugene Parta and Mark Rhodes, "Soviet Citizen Attitudes Toward Poland Since Martial Law: Agitprop, Western Radio and the Evolution of Opinion," AR 6–82, September 1982, Soviet Area Audience and Opinion Research, RFE/RL, Inc.

Section Six: Some Provisional Conclusions on the Impact of Western Broadcasting to the USSR

1. Maury Lisann, *Broadcasting to the Soviet Union: International Politics and Radio*, Praeger, New York, 1975, pp. 164–165.
2. Ibid., p. 36.
3. Ibid., p. 33, citing deputy chairman of the state committee, A. Rapokhin in "Radio, Man and His World," *Sovetskoye Radio i Televideniye*, May 1958, pp. 5–7.
4. Mark Rhodes, "Soviet TV Innovations Aimed at Reducing Western Radio Audiences," RM 1–87, Soviet Area Audience and Opinion Research, RFE/RL, Inc. April 1987. These changes consisted of greatly increasing the amount of live television programming, instituting a new "breakfast show" along the lines of "Good Morning America," and introducing a new, less formal late night news program aimed specifically at a younger audience. The main evening TV news magazine "Vremya," which had come under criticism in *Pravda* for being dull, monotonous and slow, was also revamped to make it more competitive with Western radio on international news topics. The *Pravda* article ("Vremya on the Screen: Remarks on Television News," May 19, 1986) also offered guidelines on how to tackle the problem of

providing increased coverage of the West. While calling for broadcasts describing Western technological and scientific achievements, *Pravda* noted that they should point out the lack of significance of these achievements for ordinary workers under conditions of capitalism and should highlight "problems facing women and old people and the increase in crime and terrorism in the Western world." It was now acceptable to be positive about some aspects of Western life (e.g. fast-food restaurants and the interstate highway system) but they should still be presented in a largely negative context.

Section Seven: Epilogue. A Comparison of SAAOR Findings with Data from the Archives of the Institute of Sociology of the USSR Academy of Sciences: Late 1970s and early 1980s.

1. Dr. Elena I. Bashkirova, "Measuring the Foreign Radio Audience in the USSR During the Cold War." Paper delivered at the Conference on Cold War Broadcasting Impact co-organized by the Cold War International History Project, Woodrow Wilson International Center for Scholars, Washington, DC, and the Hoover Institution of Stanford University, with support from the Center for East European and Eurasian Studies, Stanford University and the Open Society Archives, Central European University, Budapest. October 13–15, 2005. The paper will be published as part of a 2-volume publication on the conference under the auspices of the Central European University Press, Budapest, Hungary.
2. Ibid., p. 4.
3. Ibid., p. 11.
4. Ibid., p. 9.
5. Ibid., p. 9.
6. Ibid., p. 15.
7. Ibid., p. 13.
8. Ibid., p. 14.
9. Ibid., p. 15.

Appendix A: SAAOR Survey Methodology: Interviewing Soviet Travelers

1. See "The Method of Comparative and Continuing Sampling," Audience and Public Opinion Research Department, Radio Free Europe, Munich, January 1976.

Appendix C: Data Validation: Comparison of SAAOR Studies with Internal Soviet Studies

1. Mark Rhodes, "A Study of SAAOR Data Validity: Behavior and Opinion Measurement," AR 5–84, Soviet Area Audience and Opinion Research, RFE/RL, Inc. This paper was presented at the 1983 annual meeting of the American Association for the Advancement of Slavic Studies in Kansas City, MO, USA.
2. R. Eugene Parta, "Listening to Western Radio and Viewing Television in the USSR," AR 2–75, Soviet Area Audience and Opinion Research, RFE/RL, Inc. March 1975.
3. Boris Firsov, *Televidenie Glazami Sotsiologa*, Iskusstvo Publishing House, Moscow, 1971.
4. Parta and Rhodes, "Information Sources....", op. cit.
5. Mark Rhodes and R. Eugene Parta, "Attitudes of Some Soviet Citizens to Andrei Sakharov: Comparison of SAAOR Data with Unofficial Soviet Poll," AR 11–81, Soviet Area Audience and Opinion Research, RFE/RL, Inc.
6. An article describing the purpose, methodology and results of this poll appeared in the *Rheinischer Merkur/Christ und Welt* of September 24, 1981 under the pseudonym "Viktor Maxudov." A translation of this article appears in the appendix of AR 11–81.
7. R. Eugene Parta, "Andrei Sakharov and the Nobel Peace Prize." AR 2–76, Soviet Area Audience and Opinion Research, RFE/RL, Inc.
8. The results of the unofficial Soviet poll were published in the Danish newspaper, *Berlingske Tidende* of March 21, 1982.
9. Internal SAAOR memo of 27 July 1988, Mark Rhodes to R. Eugene Parta. The CBS-New York Times Poll was published in the *New York Times* of May 17, 1988 by Bill Keller: "Muscovites, in Poll, Are Split On What Their Future Holds."
10. See Mark Rhodes, "The Recent Joint Soviet-French Opinion Polls and SAAOR Data," AR 9–87, Soviet Area Audience and Opinion Research, RFE/RL, Inc., November 1987.
11. Vesevolod Marinov, "What the Comrades Say," *Time*, April 10, 1989. The sample consisted of over 1,000 residents of Moscow and was conducted March 6–14, 1989.
12. Sallie Wise, "Comparisons of SAAOR Data and *Time* Poll," Internal SAAOR memorandum, April 14, 1989.
13. Mark Rhodes, "Comparison of SAAOR Data with CBS-*New York Times* Poll," internal SAAOR memorandum, November 15, 1988. The CBS-NYT poll was conducted on 14–15 May with 939 residents of Moscow. The results were printed in the *New York Times* of May 27, 1988.

14. Alexei Andreyev, "Kto, Kak I Zachem Slushaet Radio 'Svoboda'?" (Who, How and Why Listen to Radio Liberty?), *Reiting.* No. 14, St. Petersburg, June 1992.

15. R. Eugene Parta, "Comparative Baltic Survey Figures," Internal RFE/RL memorandum from Gene Parta to William W. Marsh, June 25, 1990.

16. Radio Free Europe broadcast in vernacular languages to Estonia, Latvia and Lithuania. Radio Liberty broadcast in Russian. SAAOR conducted research in the Baltic States for both the RFE and the RL broadcasts.

SELECT BIBLIOGRAPHY

Methodology

The following monographs are available in the Audience Research Section of the RFE/RL archive at the Hoover Institution/Stanford University. The SAAOR reports referenced in the footnotes are also all available in the Hoover archives at Stanford either in hardcopy or on micro-fiche.

Dr. Ree Dawson, Massachusetts Institute of Technology. "Developing a Methodology for Projecting the Audience to Foreign Broadcasts in the Soviet Union." Summer 1986.

Dr. Ree Dawson, Massachusetts Institute of Technology. "Statistical Treatment of SAAOR Data: A Comparison of Traditional Statistical Methods and Current Audience Simulation Techniques." Summer-Fall 1987.

Dr. Ree Dawson, Massachusetts Institute of Technology. "Estimates of Geographic Audiences: Imputing Sample Values for SAAOR Interview Data." Summer-Fall 1989.

Dr. Ree Dawson, Harvard University. "Quality-Adjusted Audience Estimates: Russian RSFSR Listening to Foreign Broadcasts 1991–1992." August 1993.

R. Eugene Parta, John C. Klensin, Ithiel de Sola Pool: "The Shortwave Audience in the USSR: Methods for Improving the Estimates." *Communications Research: An International Quarterly*, Vol. 9, No. 4, October 1982.

Dr. Ithiel de Sola Pool, Massachusetts Institute of Technology. "Soviet Audiences for Foreign Radio." USIA R-17-76, September 1976. With Summary prepared by the Office of Research, United States Information Agency.

Dr. Ithiel de Sola Pool, Massachusetts Institute of Technology. "Opportunities for Change: Communications with the USSR." Paper delivered at the Workshop on Communications with the Peoples of the USSR. Radio Liberty—New York University, November 20, 1965.

MIT Communications Research Program. Dr. Ithiel de Sola Pool, Director. September 1975.

- Preface to Simulation Report Series
  1. Simulation Report #1. The Soviet Audience for Foreign Broadcasts
  2. Simulation Report #2. The Soviet Audience for Foreign Broadcasts in Minority Regions and Languages
  3. Simulation Report #3. The Soviet Audience for Domestic Media
  4. Simulation Report #4. Methodology
  5. Simulation Report #5. Trends and Variations in Soviet Audiences.

Ithiel de Sola Pool and Wilbur Schramm, eds., "Communication in Totalitarian Societies," in *Handbook of Communication*, Rand McNally, New York, 1974.

Dr. Frederick Mosteller, Harvard University. "Association and Estimation in Contingency Tables." *Journal of the American Statistical Association*, March 1968.

Maury Lisann, *Broadcasting to the Soviet Union: International Politics and Radio*, Praeger, New York, 1975, pp. 164–165.

Jamming

Pleykis, Rimantas. *Radiotsentsura*. Radio Baltic Waves, Vilnius, Lithuania, May 2002.

ABOUT THE AUTHOR
Russell Eugene (Gene) Parta

Gene Parta retired as Director of Audience Research and Program Evaluation for Radio Free Europe/Radio Liberty in Prague in September 2006.

Previously, Mr. Parta was Director of Media and Opinion Research (MOR) of the RFE/RL Research Institute in 1990. He has worked in the field of international broadcasting audience research since 1969.

During the 2007–2008 academic year he will be a Research Associate of the Institute for European, Russian, and Eurasian Studies at the George Washington University working on a book about political communication with the USSR during the Cold War.

In 2003–2004 Mr. Parta was an Osher Fellow at the Hoover Institution of Stanford University.

Mr. Parta was educated at the School of Advanced Inter-national Studies of the Johns Hopkins University (MA), St. Olaf College (BA), Harvard University and the American University. He has been a visiting research associate at the Center for International Studies of the Massachsetts Institute of Technology.

The author in the USSR in September 1990 to coordinate initial survey work in Russia, Latvia, and Ukraine.

Mr. Parta has written extensively on media use, communications and public opinion in Central and Eastern Europe and has been a frequent speaker and participant in international academic and professional conferences. He is past Chairman of CIBAR (Conference on International Broadcasting Audience Research) which unites international broadcasting audience research units worldwide.

INDEX